MAKING Animal Characters IN POLYMER CLAY

Sherian Frey

NORTH LIGHT BOOKS
CINCINNATI, OHIO
www.nlbooks.com

Acknowledgments

My deep thanks and appreciation to my husband, Carlos, for the hours and hours spent as my photographer and computer coach for this book; to American Art Clay Company, Inc. (importers of FIMO), Polyform (the makers of Sculpey) and Kemper Enterprises (importers of Cernit) for their generous assistance with clay information, tools and sample products to illustrate this book; to Greg Albert of North Light Books for asking me to do the book and Jane Friedman for serving as my editor.

Dedication

Dedicated to my family: my parents, who taught me to pay attention to details both large and small, to trust myself and to take on new challenges with determination; my husband who is my creative partner and has been my right-hand man since 1965; my two supportive sons who say "good for you, you can do this" and "go for it."

TT297
.F74
2000

04   03   02   01   00   5   4   3   2   1

Library of Congress Cataloging-in-Publication Data

Frey, Sherian.
    Making animal characters in polymer clay / by Sherian Frey
       p. cm.
    Includes index.
    ISBN 1-58180-041-X (alk. paper)
    1. Polymer clay craft. 2. Animal sculpture I. Title.
TT297.F74 2000   00-029215
731.4'2—dc21   CIP

Editor: Jane Friedman
Designer: Wendy Dunning
Production artist: Kathy Gardner
Production coordinator: Kristen Heller

METRIC CONVERSION CHART		
TO CONVERT	TO	MULTIPLY BY
Inches	Centimeters	2.54
Centimeters	Inches	0.4
Feet	Centimeters	30.5
Centimeters	Feet	0.03
Yards	Meters	0.9
Meters	Yards	1.1
Sq. Inches	Sq. Centimeters	6.45
Sq. Centimeters	Sq. Inches	0.16
Sq. Feet	Sq. Meters	0.09
Sq. Meters	Sq. Feet	10.8
Sq. Yards	Sq. Meters	0.8
Sq. Meters	Sq. Yards	1.2
Pounds	Kilograms	0.45
Kilograms	Pounds	2.2
Ounces	Grams	28.4
Grams	Ounces	0.04

About the Author

Artist/Designer Sherian Frey has been creating whimsical people, animals and houses since 1975. Her designs appear as polymer clay figures in the Small Fry Sculptures collection and also as stencils and push molds.

As a child, Sheri had a very active imagination and a supportive family that encouraged her creative growth. Favorite family outings included nature walks (looking closely at the intricacies of bugs, twigs, rocks, etc.) and museum visits. The museums visits included not only art museums but also museums of science and natural history in Kansas City, St. Louis, Denver and Chicago. There Sheri was introduced to the visual arts on a grand scale. At the age of eight she was already using modeling clay to sculpt make-believe characters to inhabit a fantasy village based on childhood stories.

Art remained Sheri's primary interest through school. After receiving an art degree from Emporia University and studying sculpture at the University of Kansas, Sheri married professional portrait artist Carlos Frey. Together they own and operate Frey Art Studio in Wayne, Nebraska.

Sheri has worked exclusively with polymer clays since 1988. Her early figures were sold through a private collector's club, which in turn opened a market for custom sculptures. Both the collector's club and the custom sculptures have been well received by the public, and Sheri has created over eight hundred individual clay designs.

Sheri has 16 years of teaching experience, and has worked with students of all ages. She spent six years teaching K-12 art classes in public schools and ten years teaching college level speech and communications, and has instructed both post-graduate and community adult education classes in art. Sheri has won numerous awards for her sculpture, pottery and painting, but is now devoting her unique talents to recreating the fantasy world that she knew as a child.

Sheri and Carlos have two sons who claim to be the original Small Frys. Chad, the eldest, is a scenic designer and art director for movies and television and lives in Burbank, California. Troy, the youngest, is a financial consultant and lives in Denver, Colorado.

Table of Contents

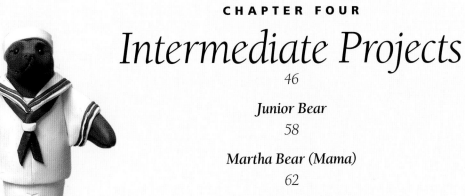

Introduction

I was introduced to polymer clay in 1988 by Maureen Carlson, author of *How to Make Clay Characters*. We were both participating artists at the Minnesota Renaissance Festival. I fell in love with the wonderful colors and ready permanence of the clay. It seemed the perfect media to use for happy, whimsical little people and animals. It awakened memories of my first clay sculptures done at the age of eight, a gathering of fairies with waxed-paper wings playing in the woods on toadstools, flowers and logs. That was a long, long time ago. How I would have loved to have had this clay then.

I'm sure those early sculptures were very crude, but they were wonderfully fun to make. Polymer clays are very well suited to creating spontaneous, happy memories.

- No special equipment or tools are required.
- Only your skill and imagination limit their use.
- They work well for beginners or professionals.
- The finished work is durable and long-lasting.

Something else I love about polymer clay is that there is usually more than one way to do something. If it works for you, go for it. The step-by-step instructions in this book show only my approach to making the projects. I started with simple projects and progressed to more complex ones to give you a feel for the clay and my technique. I recommend doing the projects in sequence, especially if you don't have much experience working with polymer clays. It is also good to remember that finesse is more effective than brute force. The more complex or detailed the project, the more delicate the handling will need to be.

There are only two rules you must obey when working with polymer clays: You must condition (soften and mix) the clay each time you work with it, and you must make sure the clay is properly cured all the way through. The package will tell you at what temperature to bake your clay. The time required to cure the clay varies with how thick it is. Generally, 15 to 20 minutes of baking time is required for each ¼-inch thickness of unbaked clay.

This book starts simple and ends with designs that are more complex. Somewhere along the way you will start getting your own ideas of things you want to do and try on your own. The fun is in the doing, the exploring, and the trying of new things. Beginners are known to make mistakes but don't let that worry you. You are allowed 10,000 mistakes. Shall we get started?

CHAPTER ONE

Clays

Polymer clay is fun and easy to work with. It is a versatile modeling material. After the clay is conditioned to make it soft and pliable, it is ready to be shaped by hand, pressed into a mold or carved with tools. It is wonderful for craft projects such as dolls or figures, miniatures, accents for the home, jewelry and holiday decorations. Polymer clays are waterproof and permanent once cured by baking in a kitchen oven.

Large objects can be made of polymer clay if supported by an armature (an internal support structure). Additional colors and layers can be added before or even after the original piece has been baked (if it hasn't been varnished). Acrylic paints, markers and many other art materials can be used to decorate baked pieces.

There are three brands of polymer clay: FIMO, Sculpey and Cernit. Each brand comes in a variety of colors that can be blended to create new colors, so infinite variations are possible. Kneading two or more colors together can create not only additional colors but also stripes or marbled effects. Each brand also offers metallic colors like silver, pewter, copper or gold, and each has a selection of colors that contain a fiber that adds strength and visual texture. FIMO and Sculpey have glow-in-the-dark clays that really do glow.

This section will familiarize you with the important characteristics that make each brand of polymer clay special. It will also help you know what you are getting and know how to substitute when you can't find the brand of clay you are accustomed to using.

This sculpture is made with a combination of polymer clays. The foxes are Premo! Sculpey, which was selected because of its color. The clothing is FIMO, selected for its strength in thin sheets and ability to hold detail. The two clays are very similar in working characteristics and in finished strength.

Cernit

Cernit is the strongest of the polymer clays once it has been baked. However, it is extremely sensitive to heat and becomes too soft to hold details except in the hands of the experienced crafter. It also loses some of its shape during baking unless supported by an armature and careful bracing; even then, it loses surface detail.

FIMO Classic

FIMO Classic (sometimes just called FIMO) is the best clay for retaining fine detail, and holds up well when the piece must be handled several times. Thin, ¹⁄₁₆-inch sheets are strong enough to be draped and folded into wonderful clothing and delicate shapes.

FIMO handles and works best at temperatures of 75° to 95° F. It is stiff and crumbles when you start to work, which makes conditioning difficult for many people. FIMO makes Mix Quick, a softener made for conditioning FIMO.

FIMO Soft

FIMO Soft handles and holds details well. It is softer than FIMO Classic and easy to condition right from the package. It does not crumble when cool like FIMO Classic and handles much like Sculpey III.

Puppen-FIMO

Puppen-FIMO is much like Cernit and is made only in two colors, Porcelain and Doll Pink. It was designed for doll makers and cures at a higher temperature than the other FIMO products.

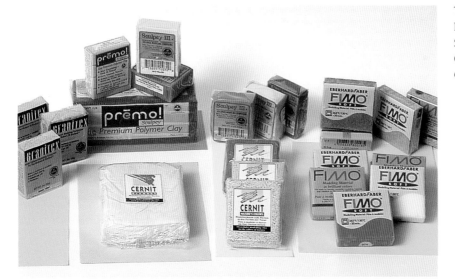

The three major brands of polymer clay are FIMO (includes FIMO Classic and FIMO Soft), Sculpey (includes Premo!, Sculpey III, Granitex, Sculpey and Super Sculpey) and Cernit.

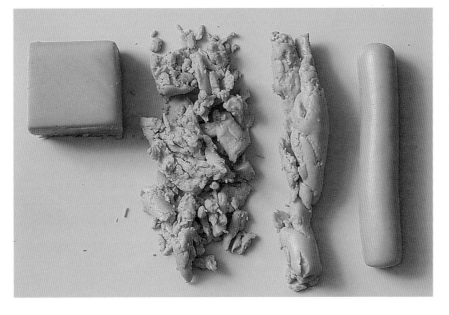

FIMO Classic is stiff and crumbles when you start to work with it, but it will soften and stick together as you continue to handle it. The older or colder the clay, the more it will crumble. Cold clay will warm as you handle and condition it. Older clay may need to have Mix Quick added to help recondition it.

Sculpey

Sculpey is the original Sculpey clay. Made only in White and Terra Cotta, it comes in a box and is the softest and weakest of the polymer clays. It is sometimes sticky-soft right from the box and suitable only for bulky projects. It does not stand up to multiple handlings or hold detail well and will "toast" or discolor during the extended baking necessary to cure thick projects. Baked Sculpey may be painted with waterbase acrylic paints.

Sculpey III

Sculpey III is easy to condition right from the package. It can be finely detailed, but loses its shape and details with multiple handlings. It can be rolled into thin sheets to fold or drape, but because the clay is softer and not as strong as FIMO, the clay sheets need to be a little thicker than those made of FIMO. This clay works best at temperatures between 60° and 80° F.

Super Sculpey

Super Sculpey is similar in strength and handling to Sculpey III. It comes in one color, a pink beige. It works well for flesh tones but darkens with prolonged baking. It can also be blended into FIMO as a softener, if you can't find Mix Quick. Do not use it as a softener for white clay because it will discolor the white and make it look dirty.

Premo!

Premo! Sculpey handles, holds details, and works much like FIMO Classic. It is stiffer and harder to condition than other Sculpey clays, but it is also stronger. It requires a slightly longer baking time than other Sculpey clays.

Super Elasticlay

Super Elasticlay, extra soft and pliable, is available in eight colors and is permanent and flexible after baking. It can be bent or stretched and will spring back to its cured shape without breaking. It is recommended for flexible one-sided molds. This is a product from Polyform, the same company that makes Sculpey.

Sculpey and Super Sculpey are the only polymer clays that are boxed. Sculpey comes in 1-lb. and 2-lb. boxes, Super Sculpey in a 1-lb. box. The other clay shown is a 225g block of Super Elasticlay.

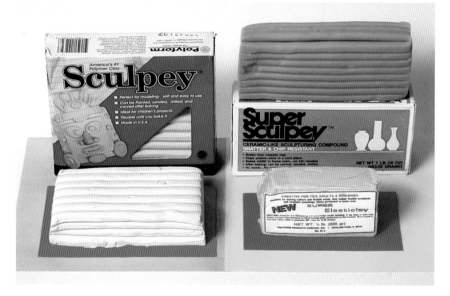

Granitex (Sculpey), Stone Colors (FIMO) and Nature Colors (Cernit)

These clays contain fibers that create a visual texture in the clay. They may be slightly stiffer or softer than other colors of the same brand. They do not cut as cleanly as clays without fibers.

Clay Softeners

Mix Quick looks like translucent white clay. It is made to mix with FIMO Classic and softens clay without changing the color. Sculpey Diluent is a clear liquid made to soften Sculpey clays.

Clay Storage

Unused polymer clay can be kept two or three years at room temperature (under 90° F) and longer if refrigerated. Freezing does not damage the clay but heat does. Do not store your clay on a windowsill or leave it in a car in the summer. Closed cars get hot enough to start the curing process and will ruin your clay.

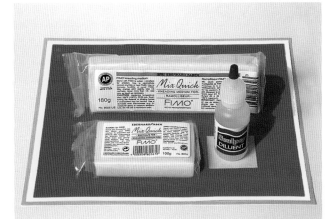

Polymer clay softeners: Sculpey diluent is a clear liquid. Mix Quick, for FIMO, comes in two sizes and looks like translucent white clay.

Clays stick together if they touch or are stacked together for awhile. Rewrap unused clay in its original packaging or in plastic. Plastic bags are great for storing clay. Put each color in a separate bag. It is not necessary to seal the bags because the clay does not air dry.

FIMO is known for retaining fine details and its strength in thin sheets used for duplicating folds in fabric. Jasmine and Jesse are 8" tall Jamaicans made completely with FIMO. Notice the details, such as toenails and teeth, clothing laces and knots, folds and ties.

CHAPTER TWO

Tools & Techniques

What are tools and techniques? They are anything that helps you achieve your goals. First you must decide what you want to do, then figure out how to do it.

You probably know more about clay techniques than you think. Most of us learned the basics in childhood when we made simple shapes like balls, cones and ropes. More advanced procedures will allow you to work larger and make complex color changes and detailed, intricate surfaces.

Your tools do not need to come from a store or be expensive. Two of my most-used tools are a round wooden toothpick and a thin-bladed paring knife that cost a quarter at the store. You will be surprised at the things you already have that will make good clay tools.

There are special tools on the market to make certain tasks easier. If you get serious about working with polymer clays, you may want to purchase them. I traded my rolling pin for a pasta machine years ago. I also use manufactured decorative cutters for many of my designs. They are great time-savers.

Work Area

You should always work on a clean surface and have clean hands. Polymer clays are soft and slightly sticky once they are conditioned, and they pick up everything! Light colors show this most. Your hands and work surface may look clean, but if your light colors soil, check again. Sometimes you even need to check what you are wearing. Sweaters and dark clothing shed tiny fibers that your clay has an uncanny way of finding.

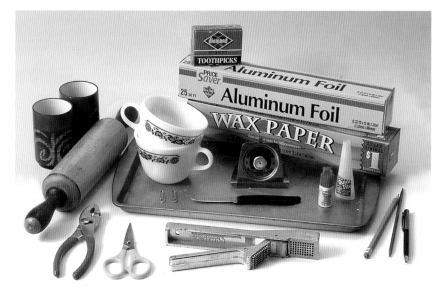

Many of the tools you need to work with polymer clays may already be in your home.

> **HOW DO I CLEAN MY HANDS?**
> If you are working with white or pastel colors be sure to wash your hands with soap and water and dry them on a white towel before you start. Moist towelettes, or a Windex-soaked paper towel will also work.
>
> If your hands are stained by pigment from the clay you may need a strong soap and a brush. Try isopropyl alcohol or baby oil and follow up with soap and water.

Conditioning

Before you actually start a project you will need to condition your clay. It must be soft and pliable. How much work that will take depends on the brand of clay you have selected.

If your clay is soft right from the package, like Sculpey III or FIMO Soft, you should still knead and twist it a little to be sure it is uniform in consistency.

If your clay is stiff, like Premo! or FIMO Classic, start conditioning it by cutting or breaking it into small, easy-to-work-with pieces. Then roll, knead and twist it until it is smooth and elastic. FIMO will crumble when you start to roll it. Premo! separates and feels a bit stringy, but does not crumble. Both will stick back together as they warm. It is easier to condition the stiff clays a little at a time. Put conditioned clay into a plastic bag and put the bag in your pocket or tuck it under your belt to keep it warm while you work on the next batch. Then knead the batches together. When these clays cool they will crumble or separate again, so to save time, keep them warm. They seem to work best when kept at 80° to 90° F. (They are easier to condition and keep conditioned in the summer.) If the clay does not soften and become plastic after several minutes of kneading, rolling and twisting, add a softener like FIMO's Mix Quick, Sculpey Diluent or Super Sculpey and try again.

Cutting With Blades

A thin blade is best whether your knife is sharp or dull—and there will be times when you want both. Soft clay is easy to cut and generally does not require a sharp blade. In fact, I dulled the blade on my most-used paring knife so that I wouldn't damage my work surface. Use a dull blade or even the back of the blade when you want a crease or a line and not a cut. A sharp knife or blade is necessary only when you are doing intricate design cuts or carving cured clay.

If you need to slice a thick piece of clay (like a mille-fiori cane) without crushing or distorting it, use a single-edge razor blade, a tissue-sliding blade from Kemper Tool or a NuBlade from the American Art Clay Company (AMACO). Be careful—these blades are extremely sharp.

Decorative cuts can be done by hand with a sharp craft knife (X-Acto) or a medical scalpel, or you can buy special cutters that are not sharp. Fiskars paper edgers and rotary cutters also work beautifully with clay sheets.

Specialized blades and cutters make many clay projects easier. Sharp knives like a scalpel or craft knife allow you to cut designs and details freehand. Shaped tools for cutting designs quickly create trims and accents from sheets of clay. Thin, extremely sharp blades cut thick pieces of clay or canes without distortion.

Measuring

If you are just playing or doing your own thing, measuring may not be of importance to you. Any ruler can be used to measure clay lengths or diameters. However, if you are following directions for a specific project in this book or mixing a new color, measuring is very important.

I used The Cutting & Measuring Template for Polymer Clays by AMACO to formulate the projects in this book and make measuring your clay easier. It has drawings on it that indicate how much clay you need to cut from your new block of clay to make various sizes of balls. There are specific drawings for both FIMO and Sculpey. It also has circle templates and a ruler for measuring reconditioned scraps from other projects. This template can be found in most craft stores that carry polymer clays.

AMACO's Marxit is a six-sided ruler designed to measure clay for beads and strips. It has ridges that instantly mark equally spaced lines when pressed into clay.

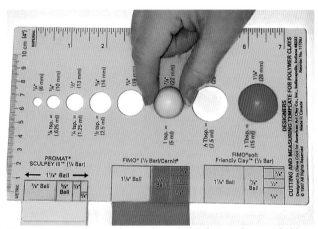

Measuring is important when making things that need to match, like beads, feet, arms, ears, or if you are mixing a new color that may need be duplicated. A common ruler will serve for many tasks, but there are specialized measuring tools to help with complex problems. A template shows how much clay will be needed for various size balls and how to measure rope diameters.

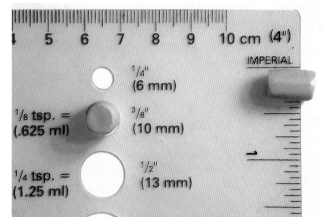

There are two ways to measure the diameter of a rope. One is to lay it across the ruler on the side of the template. The other is to place it in the circle opening.

Making Sheets of Clay

Many projects will require flat sheets of clay to create clothing or accessories. To make sheets of clay you will need some type of roller. A brayer, a small roller with a wire or plastic handle, works well to flatten small amounts of clay for use as color accents. For larger pieces, you will need a wood dowel, rolling pin or pasta machine. Start with well-conditioned clay pressed out into a patty.

Clay thinner than ⅛-inch should be rolled on waxed paper so it can be peeled off safely. Air bubbles cause problems. If they appear, puncture them and press out the air before continuing.

If you need to redo a sheet of clay, do not crumple it. That will trap air bubbles and create problems later.

Instead, fold the clay sheet in half, press any trapped air out the sides, and fold again. Always start pressing or rolling away from the fold, working toward the sides. Continue until your clay is compact enough for a fresh start.

If you are serious about your work with polymer clay, you will soon need a pasta machine. You will need one that is well made with smooth roller surfaces and gears that really align. To clean the rollers as you change from dark to light colors, simply buff the bottom of the rollers by rubbing from side to side with a napkin or paper towel. It is not wise to use the same machine for both clay and food.

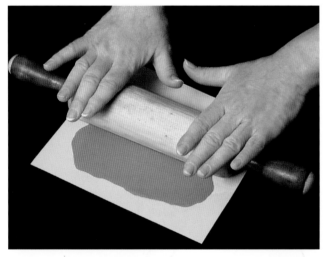

When using a rolling pin, start from the center of the clay and roll to the edge, then return to the center and roll to the opposite edge and repeat. Lift the clay, turn it and repeat the process of rolling in all directions until the clay reaches the desired thickness. This will require firm pressure. Pushing on the roller itself will save the handles from possible damage. Lift the clay sheet several times during the process to be sure it will release from the work surface.

It is important to keep your rolling pin very clean. Clay that sticks to it can transfer to other colors or attract more clay, eventually causing an uneven surface. To avoid these problems, clean your rolling pin frequently by rubbing it briskly with a soft, dry cloth.

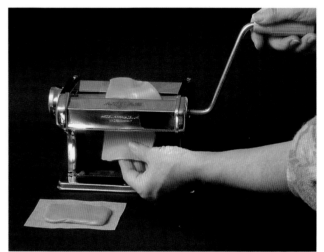

When using a pasta machine, start rolling your clay at the thickest setting. Repeat at progressively thinner settings. If you use the pasta machine to help mix clay, or if you rolled thinner than intended, fold the clay sheet in half before running it through again. Always place the fold at the bottom or side to prevent forming air bubbles.

Ropes, Balls, and Cones

As you condition your clay and it gets softer and easier to work with, try to roll a series of ropes, a round ball and a cone shape. Crush each shape back into a ball before you try the next shape; it will speed up the conditioning process. As your clay gets softer and your ropes and cones become more uniform, try opening the end of one. Insert a dowel or brush handle and use it as a roller to open the clay into a hollow shape. When you crush the hollow cone back into a ball, avoid trapping an air bubble inside.

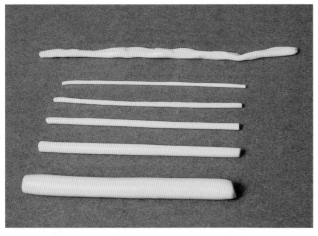

Ropes are an important element in many projects. Rolling a rope sounds easy but you will find it takes practice. Beginners usually press too hard and have their fingers too far apart, making an uneven surface (top rope). The secret is to start in the center and use light, uniform pressure as you slowly move your hands farther apart.

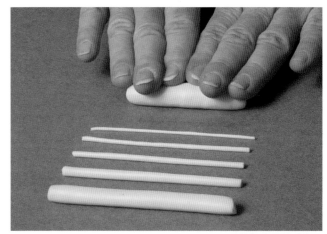

Start with a large rope and practice until you can make graduated sizes of smooth, uniform ropes. When making a large rope, use all of your fingers as you roll the clay back and forth. Start in the center, pressing gently and gradually moving toward the ends as you roll. If the rope isn't long enough, or is too thick, simply repeat the process.

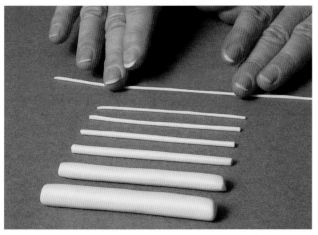

The smaller the rope, the more delicate your touch should be. Small ropes require more repetitions of rolling from the center to the ends of the clay.

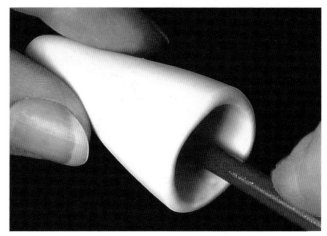

To hollow out a rope or cone, support the sides between your thumb and forefinger, and insert a brush handle or small dowel into the end. Twist the handle as you push into the clay. Lay the clay on your work surface and use the brush as a rolling pin to open the hole, alternating rolling and turning.

Extruders

Soft, well-conditioned clay can be pushed through an extruder to make distinct shapes. Two of the most readily available extruders are a kitchen garlic press and a Kemper Klay Gun.

The garlic press is the easiest to load and use, but it only makes one clay shape. The Klay Gun comes with disks to form seven different shapes, and several sizes of each shape. However, it is extremely hard to use.

Paper

Waxed paper and tracing papers have multiple uses in clay projects. Either can be used when making paper patterns. Trace the pattern, cut it out, place it on the clay and cut around the pattern to prepare the pieces necessary for complex designs. If you use waxed paper for patterns, you will need a pencil to do the tracing. Ink pens won't work on the waxed paper. Either kind of paper may be used as a support for rolled clay sheets. However, waxed paper is better for prolonged use and may be reused. Tracing paper is fine for temporary or short-term support, but will absorb plasticizer from the clay, making the clay stiffer. Loss of plasticizer "ages" your clay. Either paper may be used to band or tie your project to a support during baking. (See Papa Bear in chapter four.)

Typing paper works well for designing your own patterns. It is stiffer and easier to cut around once it is pressed onto your clay sheet.

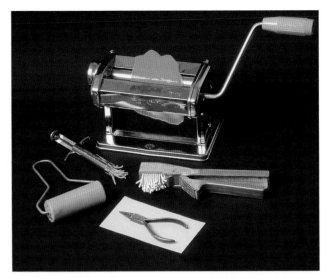

You can use a brayer (small hand roller) to create small clay sheets. Round-nose pliers are useful when making smooth curves in wire armature pieces. Clay extruders can be used to create hair, wool and decorative three-dimensional trim.

CAN I MAKE MOLDS WITH THIS CLAY?

Yes. Push molds (also called press molds) are easy to make. Begin by selecting an item of relatively low relief—that is, an item wtih no deep undercuts that will trap the clay. Dust the item with talcum powder, dust the conditioned clay, and press the clay against the item. Remove the item from the clay before baking the mold.

To use the mold, dust the inside with powder, turn the mold face down and tap to remove extra powder, press the conditioned clay into the mold, then carefully remove the clay from the mold. If the new clay sticks, try dusting both the mold and the clay with powder.

When using FIMO in a mold, it is usually only necessary to powder the mold. When using any of the Sculpey clays in a mold, it is often necessary to powder both the mold and the clay in order to remove the clay without distorting it.

Surface Detailing

You can use a variety of round, smooth objects (tooth-picks, knitting needles, upholstery pins, darning needles) to get into those tiny places your fingers just cannot reach when detailing around eyes and mouths.

AMACO makes rubber-tipped Double-Ended Clay Shapers to help smooth out tiny surface areas.

Brushes are handy to help smooth fingerprints. Designate a brush to use for this purpose only. A no. 2 to no. 5 round or filbert soft-bristle paintbrush works well for this purpose. Do not clean the clay particles from the brush after use—the longer you use the "clay brush," the more effective it will become.

Paintbrushes are also good for applying acrylic paints and sealers to cured clay. However, because the clays come in such wonderful colors, baking may be all the finishing you need.

Coloring Unbaked Clay

For subtle accents or surface color variations, use a soft hair paintbrush to apply powdered colorants like rouge, eye shadow, pastel, or chalk to uncured clay. There are also metallic powders available for this use. These powders will bake onto the clay.

Coloring Baked Clay

Baked clay can be tinted, stained or painted with water-based acrylic paints. Sealers such s Sculpey Glaze and Friendly Lacquer (by FIMO) are made for polymer clays and come in both matte and gloss finishes. Beware! Unless the sealer is formulated for polymer clays, it may react with the clay and produce a permanently sticky surface.

With these tools, you can create textures, round the corners of a mouth, smooth out finger depressions or work inside an ear. Pictured here is an old dentist's tool, a potter's cutting needle, two Double-Ended Clay Shapers, a knitting needle, smooth ¼" dowel, and an embossing tool from American Traditional Stencils.

The surface of unbaked polymer clay is slightly sticky. Any powdered colorant applied to it will stick and become fairly permanent when the clay is cured. Powdered eyeshadow or rouge will work, as will special metallic powders formulated by AMACO. After the clay is baked, it can be painted or stained with acrylic paint. Rub 'n Buff can also be used on baked clay.

Baking

Oven Thermometer

Curing at the proper temperature and for the right length of time is very important for your clay work. Since oven temperatures are not always what the oven dial implies, an oven thermometer is a must. A thermometer that sits on the oven rack or your baking tray works well.

Ovens

Your gas or electric kitchen oven can be used to bake any size clay project. Make certain your oven is preheated and set on bake (not broil or preheat) before you put your clay into it. Toaster ovens work well if your projects are small (3 to 4 inches or less).

Convection ovens are great and do not require preheating. The circulating air eliminates the hot spots conventional ovens have while heating, but you should still use an oven thermometer. I have a small, portable convection oven dedicated to polymer clay use.

Microwave ovens do not work to cure polymer clay. Polymer clays are in the plastic family, and microwaves do not affect plastics. Your microwave will think it is empty.

Baking Surface

Aluminum or glass baking sheets and pans work well. Some people use ceramic tile as a baking surface. AirBake cookie sheets are excellent. You can bake directly on these surfaces or place your clay on waxed paper, a note card or even typing paper to prevent sticking.

Curing Supports

Curing includes both baking and cooling your clay project. Clay fresh from the oven is very fragile. It appears to be flexible *but it is not*! Bending, knocking over or any attempt to reposition any part of the clay at this critical time will probably result in breakage. There are two kinds of supports for clay projects—internal and external.

Internal support (called armatures) are commonly made of wire, dowels or crushed aluminum foil. They hold your clay in place and give it more strength or bulk. An armature becomes a permanent part of the clay sculpture. It offers support during all stages.

External support is used only during curing. It can be anything used to prop or brace your clay to keep it steady during the curing process. Coffee cups, wood blocks, craft sticks or anything that will withstand the baking temperature are useful external props.

I often use both an armature and external supports when curing my projects. I'd rather be too cautious than sorry.

Curing

Proper curing is critical to the permanence of your piece. Underbaking weakens clay. If your clay is not thoroughly cured, it will eventually soften. Overbaking will darken your colors. Baking at too high a temperature will scorch the surface and cause blistering. Burning your clay will also create toxic fumes.

Baking time depends on clay thickness and the brand. Clay packages are marked with proper baking temperatures and times. Baking time is usually 15 to 20 minutes for each ¼-inch thickness of clay. If you have a solid clay head 1 inch thick attached to a large foil-filled body covered with a ¼-inch thick clay shell, you will decide your baking time by the thickness of the head, i.e. the thickest clay.

Curing may be done in stages if the item is large, thick, or uses delicate (thin or light-colored) surface decorations. Layering and multiple bakings are common for complex clay designs.

It is important to use external bracing while curing large designs, even when an armature is used. It is best to cool thick pieces in the oven. Simply turn the oven off and let the piece cool slowly inside it. This helps prevent cracks. This slow cooling process is not important for small or thin projects. However, any bracing required during curing should remain undisturbed until the piece is completely cool and safe to handle.

> **NOTE**
> I work most often with FIMO clays and usually use a lot of white and pastel colors. To insure complete curing without scorching, I deviate from package recommendations. My standard baking time is 30 minutes for each ¼" thickness of clay and I set the oven at 250° F. I have consulted with the clay manufacturer concerning this variation and have been assured the clay will cure properly. I also use a layering technique in most of my designs to protect delicate colors and details.

Clay cutters
- thin-bladed paring knife (dull)
- scalpel (very sharp)
- single-edge razor blade
- Kemper Tool pattern cutters
    heart – ³⁄₁₆" (PC5H)
    forget-me-not – ½" (PC1F)
    circles – ³⁄₁₆" (PC5R), ⅜" (PC3R), ½" (PC1R), ¾" (PCBR)
- Friendly Cutters Set #5 (AMACO)

Clay tools
- Cutting and Measuring Template for Polymer Clays (AMACO)
- ¼" wood dowel with one rounded end and one blunt-pointed end (from AMACO Polymer Clay Hardwood Tool Set) or brush handle
- Double-Ended Clay Shaper (AMACO) (TPCR #2)
- pasta machine
- garlic press
- Kemper Tool's Klay Gun
- knitting needle
- round toothpicks
- needle tools

General craft supplies
- waxed paper
- aluminum foil, thin and lightweight
- 18-gauge and 14-gauge wire
- round-nose pliers
- wire cutter
- black 3mm and seed beads
- straightedge

Paints and brushes
- Folk Art Acrylic paint, 925 Wrought Iron
- Silver-leaf Rub 'n Buff
- no. 3 and no. 7 round, soft-bristle brushes
- dark gray powder eyeshadow, powder rouge or rose/rust eyeshadow
- FIMO or Sculpey gloss polymer clay finish

GLAZES AND SEALERS
Both Polyform (Sculpey) and FIMO make waterbased finishing coats for their clays, and both provide a choice of either gloss or matte finish. Spray glazes are also useful. Krylon acrylic sprays and Blair spray glazes can be used with polymer clay, but must be applied very lightly. Do not apply more than one coat. Liquid Laminate by Beacon is a semi-gloss brush-on finish that can also be used with polymer clays.

PASTA MACHINE INFORMATION
If you use a pasta machine to make sheets of clay, this information will tell you the setting to use for the clay thickness you need. The higher the number on the machine, the thinner the sheet of clay.

No. on machine	Thickness
#1	⅛" — thickest to cover foil armatures
#4	¹⁄₁₆" — used for clothing, hat construction
#5	slightly less than ¹⁄₁₆" — used for colored trim and accents on clothing and accessories

Clays Used in This Book

FIMO Classic and the new FIMO Soft clays were used to create the characters in this book. Super Sculpey was blended into the traditional Fimo colors to serve as a softener (two parts FIMO to one part Super Sculpey).

In 2000, fifty-eight traditional FIMO colors were reduced to twenty-four, with each color reformulated and some renamed. Some of the new FIMO Classic colors are slightly different than their older counterparts. For example, the new red is lighter and brighter than the old one. You can mix colors to duplicate all of the older original colors by using mixing charts available from AMACO, Accent Import-Export, Inc. and Wee Folk Creations. Addresses are listed in the back of the book.

Matching Clay Colors

I included the generic colors you will need in each materials list. However, if you want to match the exact colors I used, you should know that I used FIMO Classic in the beginner and intermediate projects and FIMO Soft in the advanced projects. At the beginning of chapters three and four you will find listings of the Fimo Classic colors used or instructions for mixing them. In chapter five, each project lists the Fimo Soft colors used.

WHAT ARE CLAY SOFTENERS AND WHEN DO YOU USE THEM?

Under ordinary circumstances you will not need a softener. When you use one, you are introducing plasticizer into the clay, which makes it softer and moister. If the clay has been stored in less than ideal conditions, and has become somewhat dry or stiff, a softener can help.

Polyform (Sculpey) manufactures liquid Sculpey diluent. Add approximately seven drops of Diluent per two ounces of clay and work until the clay is well mixed.

Eberhard Faber (FIMO) makes Mix Quick: a soft, neutral mixing compound that is perfect for blending with crumbly or hard FIMO to make kneading easier. When used in proper proportion (approximately one part Mix Quick to five parts FIMO), colors will not be affected.

Some people mix Super Sculpey into FIMO to make it easier to condition. Use one part Super Sculpey to three parts FIMO and work until the clay is a smooth, uniform color with no streaks. When used in proper proportions and well blended there will be very little (if any) noticeable color change.

HOW DO I STORE MY LEFTOVER CLAY?

Proper storage is essential to freshness. Place clay in a plastic storage bag like a Ziploc or baggie. The clay should be stored in a cool place, unexposed to the direct rays of the sun. Refrigeration or freezing can extend the shelf life considerably.

CAN DIFFERENT BRANDS OF POLYMER CLAY BE MIXED TOGETHER?

Yes, all polymer clays have similar formulations and characteristics, so they can be mixed. However, when mixing clays together they must be VERY thoroughly mixed in order to avoid separation or layering when curing, and the baking times and temperatures should be averaged.

CHAPTER THREE

Beginner Projects for the Whole Family

The best way to learn about polymer clay is to play with it. These projects are designed to help you learn basic techniques while you have fun. The little animals do not require much clay or time so you can do them repeatedly. You could start by using only one color so you can smash it up and try again. If you use different colors and decide to redo the project, you may find the colors are difficult or impossible to separate. However, that often results in interesting marbled or striped effects that can be fun variations to the projects. You can reuse clay as many times as you want as long as you don't bake it. Remember, the fun is in the doing. You will see improvement with each new effort. These beginner projects are designed to be fun and informative without being complicated. The simplest shapes you can make are balls, ropes and cones. Let's start there, then move on to clay sheets, decorative cutters and extruders.

I USED THESE COLORS

FIMO Classic: White (0), Ochre (17), Black (9), Terra Cotta (77), Leaf Green (57), Light Flesh (43), and Orange (4)
FIMO Soft: Fluorescent Green and Indian Red

    The new FIMO Classic does not offer a gray. To make the gray used for Rudy Rabbit blend eight parts white with one part black.

WHAT YOU'LL NEED

Clay (generic color names)
• black, white, golden tan, gray, light green, dark green, red, light orange, orange
• softening medium such as Mix Quick (if using FIMO Classic)

Cutting tools
• one sharp craft knife or scalpel
• one dulled thin-bladed paring knife
• Kemper cutters:
    ³⁄₁₆" circle (PC5R)
    ¾" circle (PCBR)
    ³⁄₁₆" heart (PC5H)
    ⁷⁄₁₆" forget-me-not (PC2F), optional
• Friendly Cutter Set #5

Other clay tools
• rolling pin or pasta machine
• garlic press or clay gun
• Cutting and Measuring Template for Polymer Clay or a ruler

Miscellaneous
• 3mm black beads
• black seed beads
• sturdy brush handle or 7" length of ¼" wooden dowel, rounded on one end
• round toothpicks
• needle tools
• waxed paper
• 18-gauge copper wire
• wire cutters

Bobby Bookworm and Sammy Snail

You can tell these two are cousins because they look so much alike. Bobby Bookworm is a quiet little fellow who likes to stay home and get lost in wonderful words. To make him, follow steps 1-4 and 6. Include step 5 for Sammy, who is more outgoing. He wants to be a mailman and take all those words to other people. Haven't you ever heard of "snail mail?"

These two projects will help you get a feel for measuring and conditioning small quantities of clay; show you how to use a bead to make a smooth, round eye; and teach you to make variegated or striped clay.

Bobby Bookworm presents you with five lessons:
- measuring amounts of clay using the polymer clay template
- conditioning clay in small quantities
- rolling balls and ropes and using them in a project
- using beads for eyes
- creating a mouth

Sammy Snail uses all the bookworm techniques and introduces one additional task:
- rolling three ropes of different colors together to form one variegated color rope.

HANDLING CLAY

Warm, conditioned clay is very sensitive to pressure from your hands and fingers. When joining two clay pieces using pressure, it is better to press gently in several places than to press hard in one place. Pressing hard will deform the clay in ways you didn't intend. A gentle touch will give better and more controlled results.

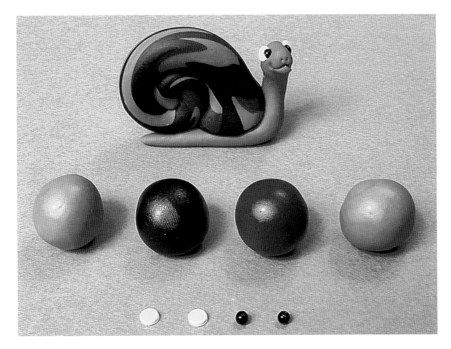

STEP 1 MEASURE YOUR CLAY

Bobby is made from:
- one ¾" ball of golden tan
- two circles cut with a ³⁄₁₆" circle cutter from a ¹⁄₁₆" thick sheet of white clay
- two 3mm round black beads

Sammy uses the same materials for his body and three additional ¾" balls (one each of golden tan, black and brown) to make his shell.

Measure your clay, condition it and roll it into a ball until you need it—except for the white. Once you condition a small amount of white, go ahead and roll it into a sheet. Put the white sheet on a piece of waxed paper.

STEP 2 MAKE THE BODY

Roll a golden tan ball into a slightly tapered rope 3½" long. Pat the blunt end of the rope with a finger to make it round and smooth before bending it to form the head.

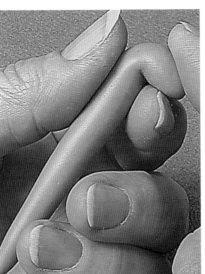

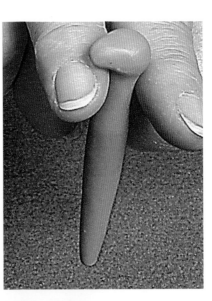

Neck. To make the neck, place your index fingers immediately under the head. Bend and roll the body rope to make it thinner than the head and middle of the body.

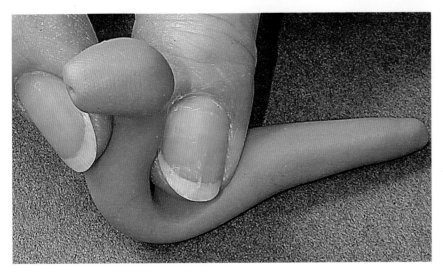

Place the body rope on your work surface and press one finger in the center to flatten the back while lifting the neck. This may be done before or after you make the face.

STEP 3   MAKE THE FACE

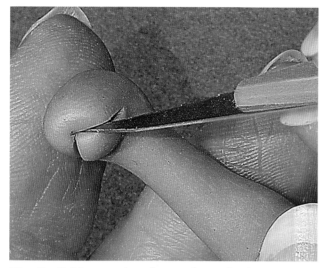

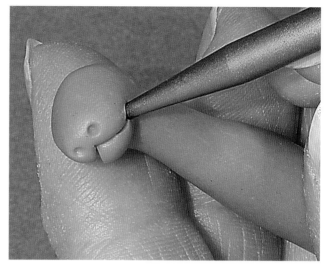

Mouth. Children can draw the mouth into the clay using a round toothpick or needle tool. Adults use a sharp knife to cut the mouth. A sharp blade produces a clean cut with minimal clay distortion. I am using a scalpel.

Use a knitting needle to round the corners of the mouth and press in nostrils.

STEP 4   MAKE THE EYES

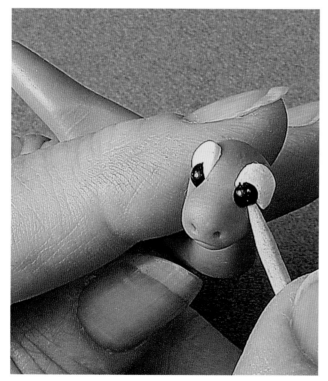

Put one white circle on each side of the head. Do not press hard; that will distort the circle's edges. Pick up a 3mm black bead on a round toothpick or needle tool to aid in placement. Push it into the nose side of the circle so no white shows between the bead and the face. Press it deeply enough into the clay so the hole doesn't show. Finish pushing it into the clay with a dowel.

MY FIMO CLAY FALLS APART WHEN I START TO USE IT. DID I GET BAD CLAY?

Polymer clays react to warm temperatures. Cool FIMO crumbles when you first work with it but will stick back together as it becomes warmed and conditioned. To speed things up, start to warm the clay before you need it. Put it in a plastic bag and tuck it under your belt or behind your bent knee to start the softening process. When the clay cools off, it will get stiff and crumbly again.

If your clay does not soften and stick back together after working with it, it has either had too much exposure to heat (left in in a hot car), or is old enough to have undergone chemical changes. At this stage, it cannot be reconstituted satisfactorily.

STEP 5 MAKE SAMMY'S SHELL

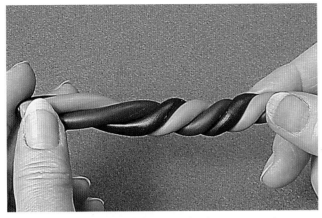

Fold the rope in half twice and work it back into a ball.

Use the remaining balls of clay to make three ropes 5" long. Stack them with two on the bottom and one on the top. Twist them together to form a striped rope.

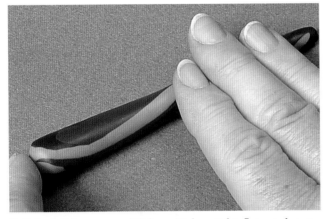

Roll the ball into a cone 4½" long. Make a tight, flat spiral starting with the small end.

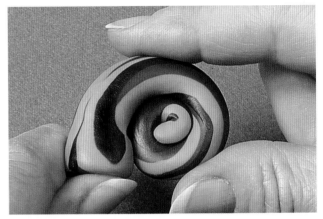

Flatten the wide end of the cone/shell with your thumb and press it onto the flattened mid-section of the body.

STEP 6 POSITION AND BAKE

Place your project(s) on a baking surface. Be sure the bottom is flat and broad enough for good support. The neck should be vertical so it won't droop during baking. Turn the head so it is facing the direction you want. The bottom of Sammy's neck can be pressed against his shell for more support. Put your project(s) in a preheated 260° F oven. If you did not use FIMO, check your clay package for the correct temperature. Bobby will take 25 minutes to bake and Sammy will need 45 minutes. They can be in the oven at the same time but put them on separate baking surfaces so they can be removed at different times. Cool before handling.

Project variations are easy—just change the colors of the clay and create a group of friendly little snails and bookworms. You can bake the whole group at the same time.

Rudy Rabbit

Rudy Rabbit presents five lessons:

- making two or more matching items: legs, feet and ears
- using beads for eyes, with bead holes exposed to the front
- applying surface detail
- creating internal support for thin or delicate shapes
- using paper patterns to duplicate shapes

STEP 1   MEASURE AND THINK IN TWOS

These are the measured clay pieces needed to make Rudy. The left side shows how the pieces were originally measured and made. The right side shows the matching pieces separated and starting to be shaped for use. When you need to make items that match, the secret is to make them both at the same time. For example, when you roll a rope for Rudy's hind leg, make it long enough for both legs and cut it in half. That way you know they will be the same length and diameter.

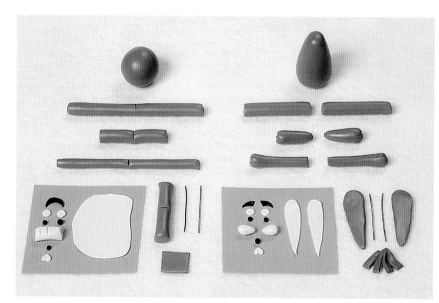

MAKING AND USING PAPER PATTERNS

Use clean white paper to trace and cut out the shape. Smooth edges are important. Place the patttern directly on your clay sheet and pat to smooth and secure it to the clay's surface. Guide your knife along the edge of the pattern, holding the knife so it will cut straight down through the clay. A thin blade will work better than a thick one.

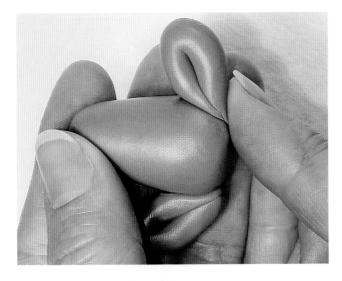

STEP 2 MAKE THE BODY AND LEGS

Make these parts:

- body – a 1" gray ball, slightly tapered into a cone 1½" long
- back feet and legs – one rope ⁵⁄₁₆" in diameter and 5" long

Cut the rope into four pieces. Two should be 1¼" long and bent in half to make the legs. Two should be ¾" long for the feet. Press the bent legs onto opposite sides of the wide end of the body cone. Notice one of Rudy's knees is closer to his body and sticks up while the other is lower and sticks out.

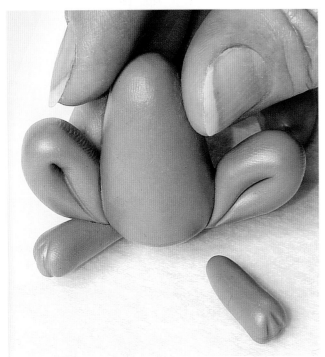

Back feet. Make the back feet by reshaping the short pieces of rope into teardrop-shaped cones ¾" long; press in place. Let the narrow end of the foot cover where the leg joins the body. Make the toe marks by rocking the side of a needle or the back of a knife blade around the end of the foot. The toes may be marked either before or after the foot is joined to the body.

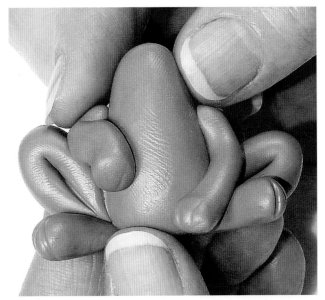

Front legs and feet. Each front leg and foot is one piece. Start with a rope ¼" in diameter and 3" long. Cut it in half and round one end of each rope for the foot. If you compress the end slightly as you round it, you will get a puffier, fuller foot. Mark the toes. One leg is fairly straight and the other leg makes a Z. Try not to flatten the top of the leg as you press it onto the body because that end of the rope makes his shoulder.

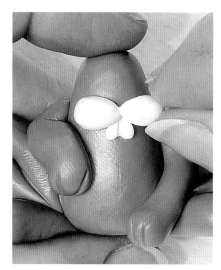

Teeth. The teeth are an inverted heart cut with a ³⁄₁₆" heart cutter from a thin sheet of white clay. Place the teeth even with the top of the arms. Use the side of a needle to press the line between them.

Cheeks. The cheeks are ⅛" slices cut from a ¼" diameter rope and rolled between your finger and thumb to make a teardrop cone.

Nose. The nose is a 3mm round bead. Use a round toothpick to put it in place and push it into the face. Angle the bead so the hole in the top is hidden in the clay.

Eyes. For the eyes, cut two ³⁄₁₆" circles from the edge of your thin clay sheet. Pick one up with the tip of your knife blade and place it on the face. Do not press it down until you have positioned both eyes and are sure they are where you want them.

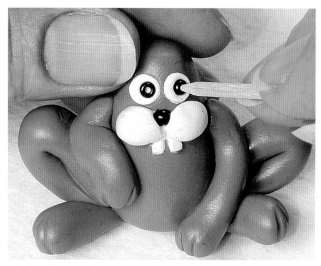

The black parts of Rudy's eyes are seed beads with the holes exposed to the front. The key to successful eyes is careful placement. First, the location of the bead within the white circle must be the same in both eyes. Second, the holes in the beads must point the same direction. If the bead's location or the direction of the hole is not the same for both eyes they won't "track" correctly and will look goofy.

Eyebrows. For the eyebrows, cut a crescent shape from a thin sheet of black clay. To do this, cut a circle with a ⅜" circle cutter. Shift your cutter slightly and cut again. Remove the extra clay around the crescent and cut it in half. You just made two eyebrows. Now pick one up with a knife blade or toothpick and place it on Rudy's face next to the white of the eye. Here the wide end is used at the top inside but sometimes I use the small end at the top for a slightly different effect.

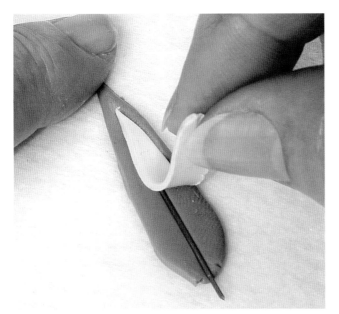

STEP 4   MAKE THE EARS

White inside. To make the white insides of the ears, roll a ¹⁄₁₆" sheet of white clay. Put the clay on waxed paper and use a knife and a paper pattern to cut two ear shapes.

Gray outside. As with most things in life there is more than one way to make Rudy's gray ears. You can start with a 1½" long, ¼" rope of clay, cut it in half and make two ear shapes. For a guide you can put waxed paper over the pattern in the book, lay your clay on it and push and pinch until the clay matches. Or you can roll out a small sheet of clay not quite ⅛" thick, make a paper pattern and cut out your ear shapes.

Wire. I am using 18-gauge copper wire 1¼" long. You can also use part of a paperclip straightened out, but no kinks or funny bends—they'll mess up your ear. Press the wire into the gray clay and cover it with the white. Notice that the wire sticks out the bottom of the ear about ¼".

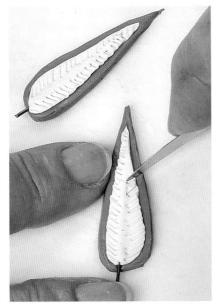

Start at the bottom of the ear and work to the tip making a series of diagonal depressions up one side with the back of your knife blade. Be careful to stay beside the wire. If you hit it, the wire will show. Apply texture on both sides of the wire. This texturing has two functions: it secures the wire by bonding the two colors of clay; and it adds visual interest to your project.

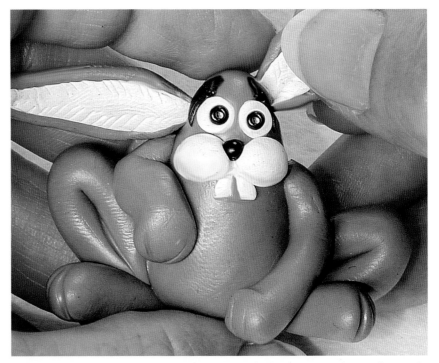

Before attaching the ears, determine the angle at which you want each ear. Then push the wire into the head until you can press the clay of the ear onto the head. If you crush out some of the details, support the back of the ear with a finger and repair it.

Ear shapes.

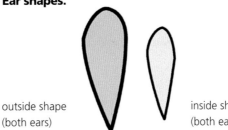

outside shape
(both ears)

inside shape
(both ears)

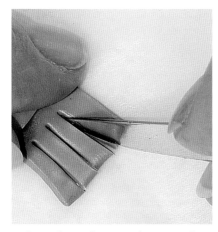

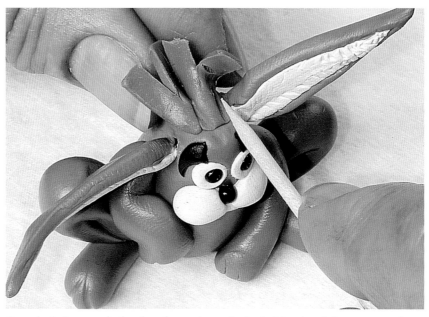

Hair. Rudy's topknot is a three-strand fringe of clay cut from a ½"-wide strip of gray. Pick up the fringe and pinch the joined ends together enough to fit between his ears.

Press the hairs onto the head so they point to the back. Now bend them over so they cover where they are joined to the head. Stick the ends to the head to give them more stability.

Tail. Make a ¼" ball of white to press on Rudy's tail. It can be left smooth or textured with the back of your knife like the paws. Once the tail is on, it is time to make final adjustments and bake for an hour in a preheated 250° F oven.

Variations on a theme. Just follow the same basic directions, only change clay color, ear directions and leg positions to create a whole family.

CAN I MAKE CHANGES ONCE THE CLAY IS BAKED?
Yes. Baked clay may be further worked by carving, sanding, drilling, or adding more clay and re-baking. When carving, drilling or sanding your cured clay, hold the item firmly, but be careful not to crush delicate areas. Make sure to aim the tip of the cutting tool away from yourself. Newly worked areas will change in color because a hand-smoothed or tooled surface looks different from a cured, cut surface.

Freddie Frog

Freddie Frog presents three new lessons:
- using decorative cutters
- making a more complex foot
- making eyes with clay

Here are the parts you will need to create Freddie. Make them as you need them so the clay will be soft and flexible when you use it. Exception: make a sheet of clay with ¼ block of bright green clay. Roll it to ¹⁄₁₆" thick and lay it on a piece of waxed paper. Cut the pieces you will need from this sheet as you need them.

> **IF THE CLAY IS SOFT RIGHT OUT OF THE PACKAGE CAN I JUST GO AHEAD AND USE IT?**
>
> All polymer clays should be properly conditioned (kneaded manually or passed through the rollers of a pasta machine several times) before use. Failure to condition the clay can result in a weak finished product and an increased chance of breakage. Thorough conditioning and mixing is particularly important when combining different brands of clay.

Frog parts

foot pad
(use for both feet)

tummy shape

STEP 1   MAKE THE BODY

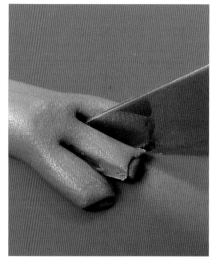

You will need one ¾" ball of green and one ¾" circle of bright green cut from the sheet of clay using a knife and paper pattern or a ¾" circle cutter. A dull, thin-bladed knife will work to cut the circle. Place the circle on the ball and press it in place. Start at the center and work out to avoid trapping air bubbles. The light green circle is Freddie's belly.

STEP 2   MAKE THE BACK LEGS

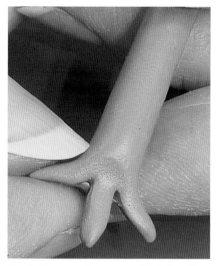

Make a rope of green 5" long and ¼" in diameter. Cut the rope in half; be sure to measure because each half will make one back leg. Slightly flatten both ends of each piece. Make two cuts with a dull knife on one flattened end of each leg for toes.

Feet. Separate the toes and lightly roll and pat each one to round and smooth the cut edges. The toes may become longer as you taper and smooth it. If they get too long, tap the end to compress and shorten them. Bend the end of the leg just above the toes to make the foot. Now bend the leg in half with toes and foot pointed out.

HOW TO USE DECORATIVE CUTTERS

Friendly Cutters look and work like little cookie cutters. Place your fingers across the top and push straight down. If the clay sticks in the cutter push it free with a blunt dowel or brush handle.

Kemper cutters work best if held by the cutting cylinder. Holding the spring plunger will not provide the stability necessary for clean cuts. Press straight down. Use the spring plunger to free clay lodged in the cutter.

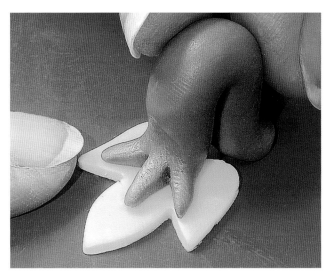

Foot pad. Use the small leaf cutter from the Friendly Cutter set to cut the foot pad from your sheet of light green clay. (You could also use a paper pattern and knife.) Spread the toes, center the foot on the pad and press to stick them together.

Press the leg onto the body with the toes pointed out. Allow enough room between it and the belly spot for the front leg. Use a dowel or brush handle and roll the joint to ensure a good bond. Repeat for the other back leg.

STEP 3   FRONT LEGS

Slightly flatten the center of the leg rope and press it onto the top of the body. Wrap the legs around the belly circle and press into place.

The front legs are one rope with a foot at each end. Make the green rope 3" long and ³⁄₁₆" diameter. Make the toes and foot bends following the same steps used for the back feet. The foot pads are made with the ⁷⁄₁₆" forget-me-not cutter. Arrange the toes on three flower petals. Center the middle toe and line up the outer toes along the outer edge of their respective petals. The other two petals will be covered by the foot and won't show.

STEP 4   MAKE THE HEAD AND MOUTH

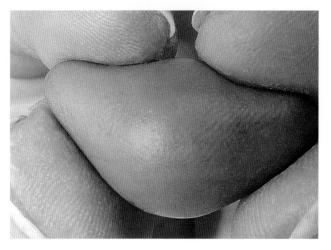

Head. Roll a ⅝" ball of green into a football shape 1" long. Press your index fingers into the top while curving the ends up with your thumbs.

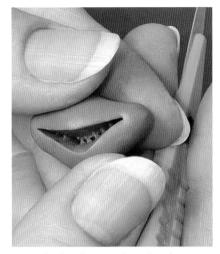  

Mouth. Cut the mouth with a sharp knife. Open the mouth by placing a thumb on each side and moving them apart. Use a knitting needle to round the corners of the mouth and press in the nostrils.

Tongue. Flatten a ⅛" ball of red clay between your thumb and index finger. Roll the clay around a round toothpick and press into the mouth. Press down and roll the toothpick from side to side to stick the tongue in place.

Press and wiggle the head onto the body until it sticks. Use a wooden dowel to deepen the finger groves on top of the head.

STEP 5 MAKE THE EYES

Make two ¼" balls of the lighter green. Use a small dowel or brush handle to cup each ball and attach to the head.

Make two ¼" balls of white. Cut two ³⁄₁₆" circles of ¹⁄₁₆"-thick black using a circle cutter. Press the black circles onto the white balls and fit them into the eye cups on the head. Press the eye cups to fit and hold the eyeballs in place. Bake Freddie for 45 minutes in a preheated 265° F oven. Remember to let him cool before handling. The eye balls with black circles can be baked before placing them in the eye cups.

Lacy Lamb

Lacy Lamb presents you with one new lesson: using extruders. Lacy Lamb's job is to let you experience using a clay extruder—either a clay gun or a garlic press. The clay gun will require using soft clay like Sculpey III or FIMO Soft. To use regular FIMO you will have to add softener. Garlic presses come in different shapes and sizes and work with any of the polymer clays. They are also easier for little hands to load and work. For this project, I used a common kitchen garlic press. Some presses (mine, for example) let the clay leak out in places other than the extruding holes. If your press has this problem you will have to gather up the "runaway" clay, press it back into a lump and try again. Lacy Lamb needs all the wool she can get.

STEP 1   MEASURE YOUR CLAY

To make Lacy you will need two ⅞" balls of clay and two 3mm black beads.

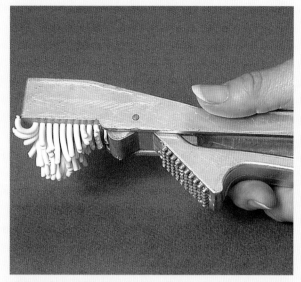

Place soft, conditioned clay into the press and squeeze the handles together. For short pieces squeeze a little. For long pieces squeeze a lot. For longer pieces squeeze, add more clay and squeeze again.

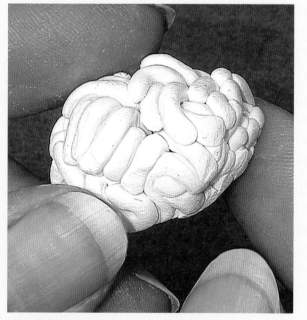

Remove the clay by sliding a dull knife blade along the surface of the press. The cut clay will stick together and to the knife blade.

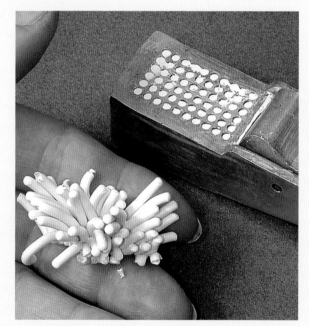

Carefully lift the clay from your knife.

Extruded clay is delicate, so handle it gently as you press or pat it into shape.

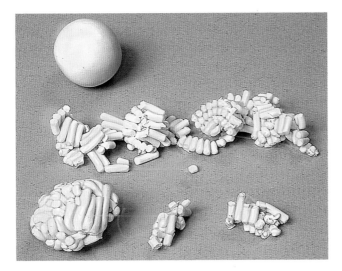

STEP 2 MAKE THE BODY

Lacy's body is made from extruded clay. Use a garlic press to make the white ball into as much extruded clay as possible. The bottom row in the photograph shows most of the extruded clay formed into an oval body and two smaller groups that will be used on the head and tail.

STEP 3 MAKE THE LEGS

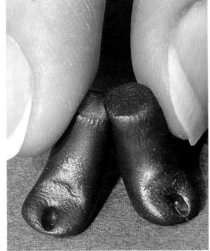

Roll the black ball of clay into a rope 4½" long and ¼" diameter. Cut four pieces ¾" long and save the rest of the rope for later use. Round one end of each leg and use a finger to make a slightly sloping foot bend.

Make two pairs of legs by pressing the tops of two legs together. Use a pointed tool (a round toothpick, needle, or knife) to press or cut the hooves.

Attach the legs by pressing them onto the body. Use a tool to pull white clay around the top of the legs.

STEP 4 MAKE THE HEAD

Cut a 1" piece of the remaining black rope. Roll it into a ball, then into a teardrop shape. The easiest way to make the teardrop is to place the ball of clay in the palm of your hand and roll it with one finger of your other hand. Next use 3mm black beads for the eyes. Use the bead on its side and press it deep enough into the head to hide the hole.

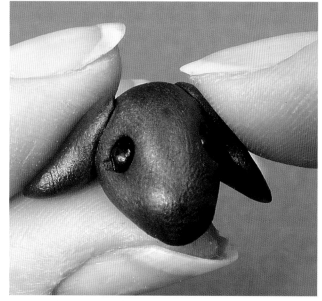

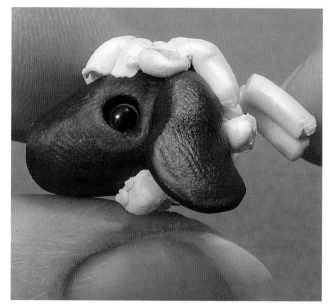

Ears. Cut two ¼" slices from the last of your black rope and make two flat teardrop shapes. Make the narrow end thicker for the top of the ear. Attach the ears to the head.

Woolly head. Attach short pieces of extruded clay to the top, back and bottom of the head before pressing it onto the body. Pull and press the strands of clay around the neck with a knitting needle or pointed tool to secure and hide the joint.

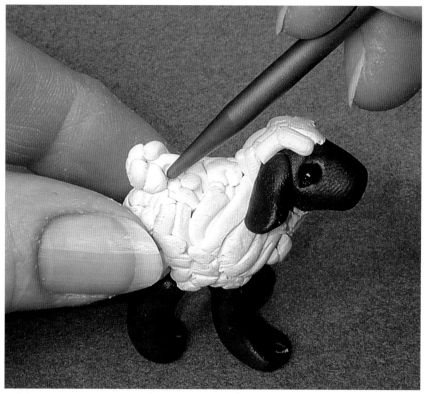

STEP 5   FINISH LACY

Make a ball of extruded clay. Place it on Lacy's rump and use a pointed tool to push and pull the clay strands together. Use any remaining extruded clay to fill low spots in the body, especially under the chin.

Put on a baking surface. Check the angles of her head, ears, legs and feet. Place in a 250° F preheated oven and bake 45 minutes. Cool before handling.

Louie & Louise Lion

Louie and Louise Lion follow all the same steps except the last one, where Louie gets a flowing mane and a tassel on the tip of his tail. King Louie presents three new lessons:

- a new approach to measuring things that are made in pairs; most of Louie's duplicate parts start as measured balls that are cut in half and slightly reshaped.
- making a complex part and then joining it to another piece; Louie's muzzle is made of four separate pieces that are joined as a unit and attached to his head.
- cutting, curling and "combing" hair; become a hairdresser for a king! It's not often you get to comb a lion's mane.

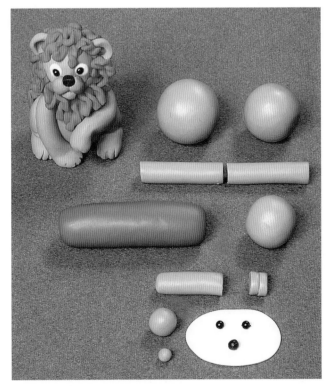

STEP 1   MEASURE YOUR CLAY

Here are the basic pieces needed for Louie, as shown from top to bottom. Except as noted, make the pieces from light orange (FIMO Classic Light Flesh) clay.

- body – 1" ball
- back legs – ⅞" ball; front legs – 2½" x ¼" rope
- mane and tail tassel – rope made from ¼ of a block of orange
- head – ¾" ball
- tail – 1" x ¼" rope
- ears – ¼" x ¼" rope
- muzzle – ⅜" ball
- chin – ⅛" ball
- nose – ⅛" ball (black)
- eyes – two 3mm black beads and a ¹⁄₁₆" thick sheet of white for cutting eye circles. The eye and nose pieces are laying on the white so you can see them better.

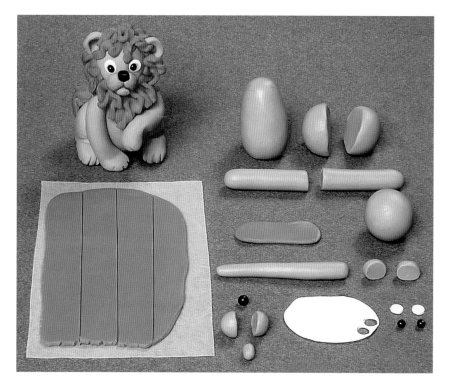

Adjust the pieces as follows:

- Roll the body ball into a slightly tapered 1½" oval.
- Cut the balls for the back legs and muzzle in half.
- Cut the front leg rope in half and round the paw ends.
- Taper and shape the tail to 1¾" and cut the ears.
- Cut white circles for the eyes using a ³⁄₁₆" circle cutter.
- Roll the block of orange for the mane and tail into a sheet of clay almost twice as thick as the white (#4 on a pasta machine). Place on waxed paper and cut into ½" wide strips. Wait until you need it to make the sheet for the mane so the clay will be warm and flexible.

STEP 2   MAKE THE LEGS

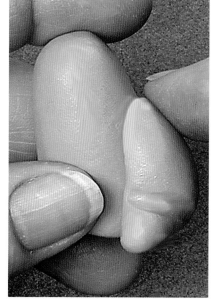

The front legs, tail and ears are made from a ¼" diameter rope of the same color. To insure accurate measuring, make one long rope and blunt one end by trimming with a thin-bladed knife. Measure from the flattened end and cut the needed pieces. First, cut ⅛" slices for the ears, then cut the other parts from the remaining length.

Back leg. The leg and foot are made from the same piece of clay. Use one half of the ⅞" ball for each leg. It should remain round on one side and flat on the other. Make the foot by gently pinching about one third of the edge then rolling it between your finger and thumb to form a short rope projection.

Next, pinch and press the top of the leg so it thins slightly. This will make the leg grow a little taller. Attach the flat side of the leg to the body by rolling your finger from the thickest part of the leg to the edge. Repeat this until there is no crack between the body and the back half of the leg.

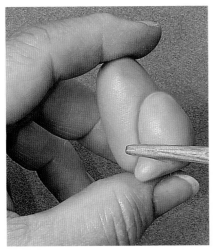

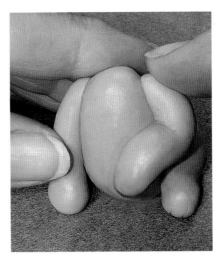

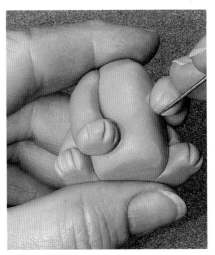

Emphasize the crease between the leg and the foot by rolling a round toothpick or brush handle around the lower leg. To do this properly you must hold the tool diagonally in relation to the body. Start pressing the crease by placing only the tip of your tool on the inside of the foot. Then roll from the tip of your tool down its side. By rolling diagonally around the leg and from the tip down the side of your tool, you will preserve the round shape of the leg.

Front legs. The front legs and foot are made from the 2½" x ¼" rope, cut in half and rounded at both ends. Compress one end slightly to enlarge it for the paw. One leg is only gently curved. The other leg is a modified Z shape. Press the legs onto the body. Use a rolling finger motion so the end of the rope stays rounded, forming the shoulder.

Mark the toes into each paw by pressing and rolling the side of a needle over and around the end.

STEP 3   MAKE THE FACE AND HEAD

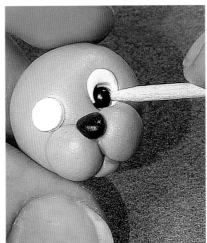

Muzzle. Roll each half of the ⅜" muzzle ball into a ball and lightly press them together. Next roll the ⅛" chin ball to flatten the center and make a short rope with a rounded end. Roll the nose ball between your thumb and finger to warm it. Now put the nose on one side of the muzzle balls and the chin rope on the opposite side and press just hard enough to hold them together. Attach the muzzle to the face.

Use a knife blade to lift the white eye circles and place them on the face. Put them about one eye-width apart. Pick up a 3mm bead on the end of a round toothpick and push it into the bottom half of the white circle, setting it on its side so the hole won't show. Place it low enough in the circle that no white shows between the bead and the muzzle.

Ears. Cup each slice of ear rope using a rounded wooden tool, such as a dowel or brush handle. Use it to position and attach the ear. Attach the head to the body and position it. If you are making Louise (the lioness), skip to the last step to make and attach her tail. Remember, no tassel for her tail.

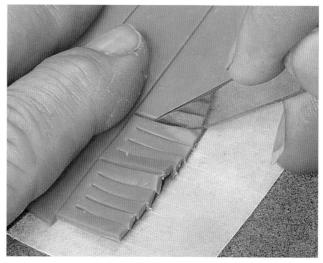

King Louie's mane is made from a sheet of orange clay that is thicker than that used for the whites of the eyes. Place your sheet of clay on a piece of waxed paper for easy handling. Use a straightedge and knife to trim one edge. Cut the sheet into ½" strips. Cut the first strip into a fringe with ⅛" wide strands. The exact width is not important, so don't take time to measure it. I usually work with five-strand sections, but some places only need one, two or three strands. Be flexible. This is hair, and it dictates its own needs to fill the allotted space.

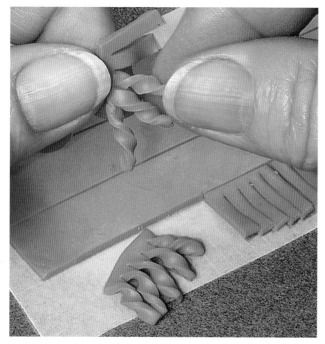

Pick up one section of clay fringe by the connected side. Now separate and twist each strand to curl it. You can curl as you go, or do several groups at once. If the clay is too cool, it will break when you curl it. Hold it between your hands for a little while to rewarm it. To keep it warm until you are ready to use it, place it between two layers of waxed paper, lay it on your thigh and cover it with a cloth towel.

Start applying hair at the bottom and work to the top of the head. That way each new row hides where the preceding one was attached. Once a section of hair is in place, use a round tool to roll the edge onto the body or head. Louie's first fringe looks like a collar.

The second row of hair starts with three strands attached under his chin where the chin and head meet. They should stick straight out (forward). That is so you can get between the layers to roll the edge onto his chin/throat. Once that is done, bend the hairs down to meet his chest hairs. Next do his cheeks and work around his head. The cheek and back hairs hang down and are rolled onto the head like the first row. Continue cutting, curling and layering the back of his head all the way to the top.

The hair surrounding Louie's face is attached with the strands pointing forward so the edge can be rolled and then hidden by bending the hairs back away from the face. Use a toothpick or needle tool to arrange individual hairs. Cheek hairs and the single row in front of the ears outline the face rather than being attached horizontally. Also remember the effect of gravity and let the hairs angle back and down into the rest of the mane. Be sure his ears remain visible.

Make the hairline on his forehead slightly V-shaped. Start in the center and go back to the top edge of each ear. Fill in the top of his head and attach the last group of hairs pointed away from their final direction so they can be bent back to cover their rolled edge.

STEP 5   MAKE THE TAIL AND FINISH

Do your final "combing" and arranging of the mane.

Wrap the small tip of Louie's tail with a five-strand fringe of hair, either curled or straight. Shape the tassel.

Attach the tail to the body, and loop it into a big curl that rests against his back and leg. Attach the full length of his tail to his body. This will keep it from getting broken easily.

Make final adjustments to Louie. Place him on a baking surface and into a 250° F oven to bake for 1 hour. Cool before handling.

CHAPTER FOUR

Intermediate Projects

Now that you've done the beginner projects and have experience working with the clay, you're ready to advance to more complex projects.

As clay items become larger, they usually get thicker too. If your clay gets too thick (¾-inch or more), it will be difficult to cure without causing discoloration and cracking. In this chapter we will explore two ways to avoid those problems: one is using a technique called "layering" and the other is to build bulk or thickness with a crushed foil armature.

Layering simply means you start with a small shape, cure it (bake and cool), add another layer of clay, cure it and so on. The process repeats until the shape is as large as you want. This technique ensures that the clay completely cures without the cracking or discoloration that may result from a long bake or a too-thick build of raw clay.

Layering is also useful if you have a large (thick or bulky) shape that has delicate (thin or light-colored) surface details. The thicker part of the project can be cured for its longer baking time before adding the more delicate surface details. This type of layering is used when making Mama or Papa Bear in this chapter. I should caution you that unbaked clay sticks easily to unbaked clay, but it is not as willing to stick to baked clay. It may take a little more effort on your part, or even a tiny bit of super glue to get started.

If you are building your base shape in layers, don't cure the final layer before adding the finishing details.

All layers do not have to be the same thickness. The real function of a top layer could be to provide an easy-to-work surface, rather than to build bulk, so it can be thin.

If you use this bake-as-you-go technique, you can remove the top unbaked layer or layers and not lose the whole project. If things are not going the way you want, take unbaked layers off and try again.

The second way to avoid getting your clay too thick is to use a crushed-foil armature. Use an inexpensive, lightweight aluminum foil. The lighter it is, the better because it will easily compress and work into a smoother surface. Create your basic shape in crushed foil, then cover it with one or more layers of clay. The foil will give bulk and strength while saving on baking time, weight and clay. Be sure the clay not only covers the surface of the foil, but is thick enough to fill grooves and pits without thinning.

Sometimes a second or third layer may be necessary to provide the surface and thickness needed for a strong project. How many layers you need depends on the project size, the thickness of layers, and any additional weight the clay shell must support. For the projects in this chapter you will need a single ⅛-inch layer.

To make the bear family, you need to start with some general information on making and covering a foil armature for the body, shaping a head and texturing. Each bear is a different size, which is listed with the individual projects.

General Bear Instructions

MAKING FOIL ARMATURES

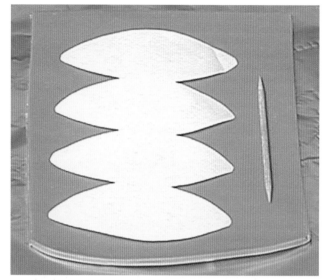

The basic things you need for preparing the body are light-weight aluminum foil, a sheet of clay and a paper pattern.

A controlled crumple will give you an easier shape to work with. Start by placing your fist in the center of the foil and cupping the foil around it.

Next, place the foil between your hands and use your fingers to close the edges together as you gently compress the foil into an egg shape. Gradually rotate the foil as you compress it by working it back and forth between your hands. Continue this process until you almost reach the size you will need.

Use your fingertip to press down high places or rough spots and smooth the surface as you finish compressing the foil into the size and shape you want.

COVERING FOIL ARMATURES

Trace and cut out the appropriate paper pattern to go with your project and place it on a freshly-rolled sheet of clay (⅛" thick). Hold the knife straight up and down for a clean vertical cut. (I used a dull paring knife).

Curl the cut clay around the egg so the edges meet but do not overlap, and press them together. If the clay is loose around the foil, gently squeeze and compress until it fits. If it doesn't reach all the way, add a strip of filler cut from scraps of the clay sheet.

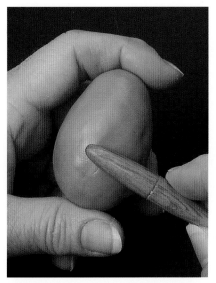

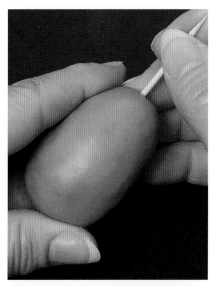

Close the clay over the ends of the foil and press the seams together. Leave the hole in the tip until you are finished smoothing the surface (next photo) so air won't be trapped inside. Start at the center of the egg and work toward the ends, pressing the clay onto the foil to fill crevices and pushing out trapped air pockets.

Roll the surface with a dowel or brush handle to remove push marks or irregularities and seal the holes at the tips.

Insert a round toothpick into the narrow end of the egg leaving only one-third of it showing.

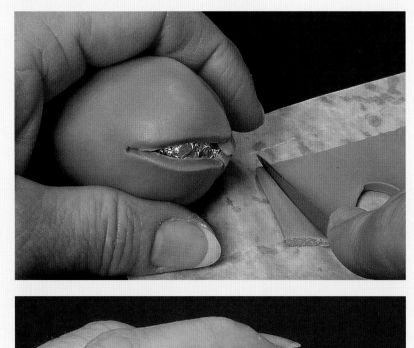

If there are gaps in the clay after you have fit the piece over the foil, cut pieces from the scraps of clay left over from the ⅛" clay sheet.

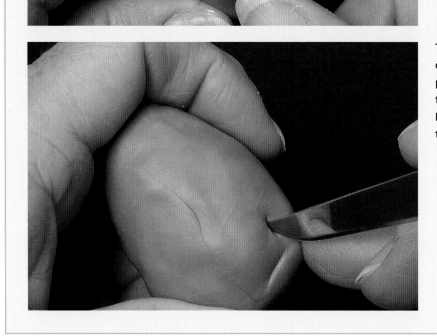

To remove air bubbles, make a small cut through the clay and then roll or push from the outside of the bubble toward the cut, forcing the air out. Do this from all sides before resealing the cut.

MAKING ARMS

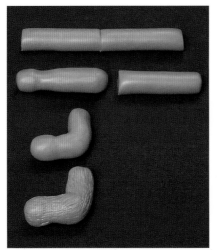

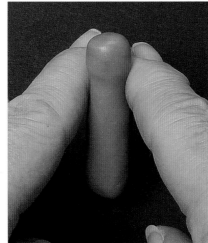

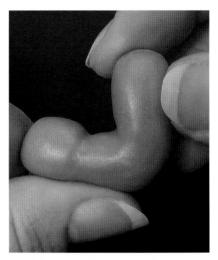

Roll a rope the diameter needed and long enough to make both arms. Cut it into the desired lengths. Round the ends of both pieces.

Roll the rope between your fingers to form the wrist.

Bend the arm at the center using your thumbs to establish an L shape.

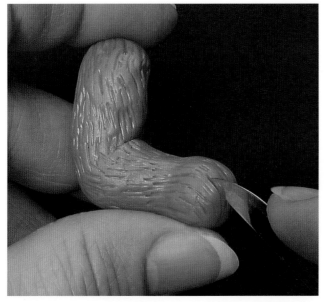

To texture the bear so it looks hairy, use a dull paring knife, a round toothpick or a large needle (not a knitting needle) to press in the hairs. Make short strokes that follow the length of the piece.

HINT
Texturing may be done piece-by-piece as you go or after the bear is assembled. It is easier for beginners to add texture before assembly because the individual shapes are easier to work with.

MAKING LEGS

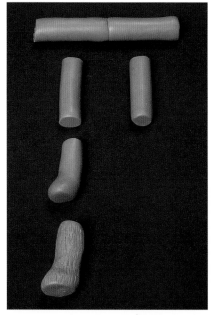

Roll a rope the diameter needed and long enough to make both legs. Cut it into the desired lengths and round the ends of both pieces. Make the foot as shown below. Texture the surface.

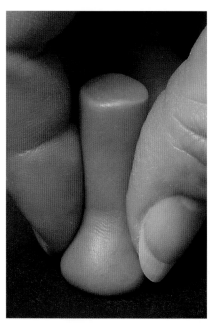

Hold the leg at the ankle. Support it on the sides and back with your fingers as you press down and back to form the foot.

MAKING HEADS

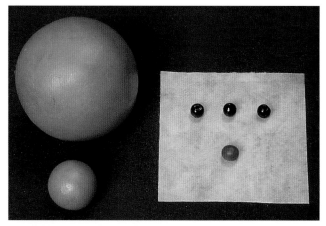

The basic bear head is make with six parts: three balls of clay (large for the head, small to be cut in half for ears, and tiny for a tongue) and three beads (all the same size, for eyes and nose).

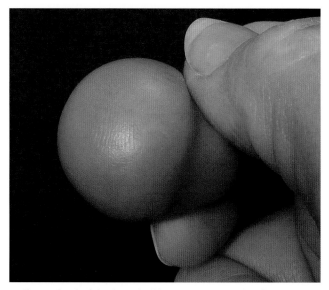

Roll one-third of the large ball between your index finger and thumb to create a mushroom-like shape.

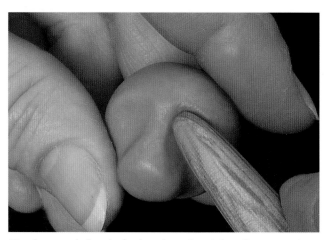

Use the rounded end of a dowel or a brush handle to press in eye sockets and roll the top edges of the snout.

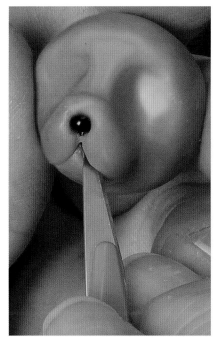

Use a round toothpick to press the nose bead in place. The toothpick will make a groove under the nose showing where to start the mouth cuts. Use a sharp knife for a clean cut.

Place the bead eyes, holding the toothpick to the side to make groove marks at the corners of the eyes. Open the mouth enough to insert the tongue. The tongue is made by flattening the tiny red ball between your finger and thumb. Wrap it around the end of the toothpick and press it in place.

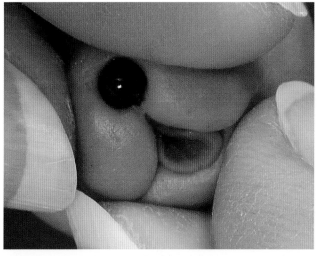

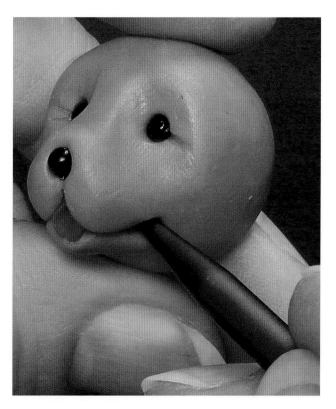

Close the mouth, then use a knitting needle to round and smooth the corners.

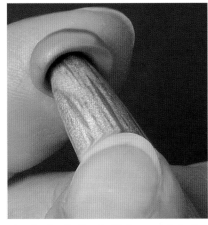

Cut the last ball in half. Form each half into a small cup and press it into the head. Buff the seam away with your fingertip.

HINT

When joining two pieces of clay, use a finger or a rounded tool to press and roll the area to cover the seam. Then lightly buff the surface with your fingers to smooth it. If you have textured your bear, it will be necessary to redo some of it where you have pressed during joining. Texturing is a great way to hide the seams.

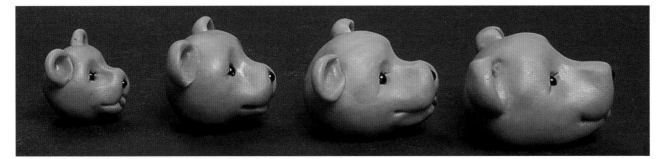

Our bear family has four members. Their heads are very similar, but the nose gets longer and the jaw becomes deeper and fuller as you progress from baby bear to Papa.

Curing Large or Thick Projects

It will take 1 hour and 20 minutes at 250° F to cure the heads of the three larger bears. That is too long for the light colors of Papa Bear's hat and vest, Mama Bear's apron or the bubbles in Junior's tub. The solution is to do a long bake first for the thick areas and a shorter bake later for the thin areas and light colors. In other words, you will be layering.

It is necessary to use external bracing while curing large or delicately balanced projects. Bracing is important to provide support during baking because your clay will become too soft to support itself. You can do this in two ways: by propping things against the clay, or by strapping the clay to a support with a strip of waxed paper and a paperclip. It is best to cool thick pieces in the oven to prevent cracks. For small or thin items, this slow cooling is not important. However, any bracing required during baking should remain in place and undisturbed until the piece is cooled completely and safe to handle. Directions for bracing will be shown with each project.

I'M HAVING PROBLEMS WITH BREAKAGE AFTER THE CLAY IS BAKED. WHY?

Breakage may indicate that the clay has been undercured. Curing times given on the clay package should be increased for each ¼" of thickness of clay. Example: the package may say 265° F for 15 minutes. If your piece is ¾" thick at the thickest place, you will need to bake three times longer, or 45 minutes.

HOW CAN I FIX A CRACK IN MY CLAY?

If a crack develops during baking, it can be filled with the same color of clay and re-baked.

CAN THE CLAY BE BAKED MORE THAN ONCE?

Yes. If a project is going to be very thick (over ¾") when finished it should be made in layers. Each layer should be cured/baked to prevent cracking in the final surface. Baking in stages also allows you to harden bulk or structural forms for safer handling while adding final surface details in fresh clay.

WHAT YOU'LL NEED

Clay (generic color names)
• golden tan or light brown, medium brown, silver/gray, red, white, blue, light blue, dark brown, green and yellow

Cutting tools
• one sharp craft knife or scalpel
• one dull, thin-bladed paring knife
• Kemper cutters:
    ³⁄₁₆" circle (PC5R)
    ⅜" circle (PC3R)

Clay tools
• Cutting and Measuring Template for Polymer Clays or ruler
• garlic press or clay gun
• rolling pin or pasta machine

Miscellaneous
• 3mm black beads and seed beads
• metal bottle cap
• round toothpicks
• knitting needle
• sturdy brush handle or 7" length of ¼" wooden dowel, rounded on one end
• lightweight aluminum foil
• waxed paper
• tracing paper (optional)
• Silver Rub 'n Buff (optional)

I USED THESE COLORS

FIMO Classic: White (0), Ochre (17), Black (9), Terra Cotta (77), Leaf Green (57), Red (2), Golden Yellow (15), Blue (37)
FIMO Soft: Indian Red

The new FIMO Classic does not offer a gray. Blend eight parts white with one part black or use Fimo Soft Metallic Silver. The Dove Gray originally used for Papa Bear's vest is no longer offered, but it can be made by blending six parts white, one part blue and one-half part black.

Mama's patterns

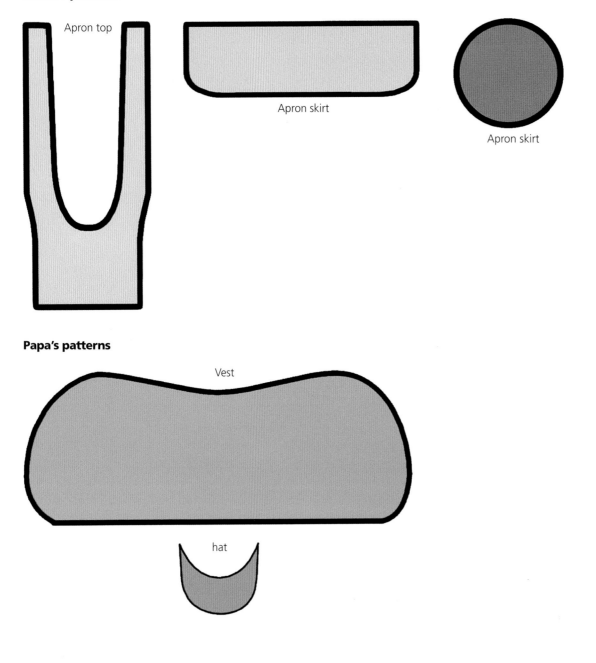

Apron top

Apron skirt

Apron skirt

Papa's patterns

Vest

hat

Papa Bear's body

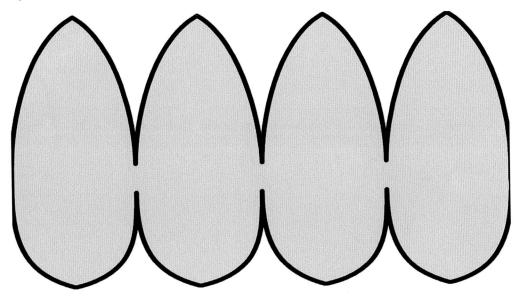

Mama Bear's body

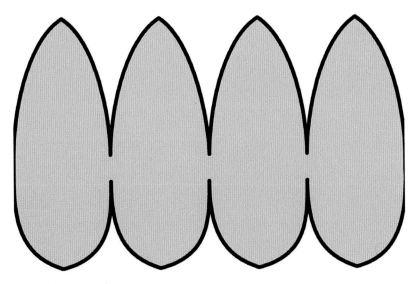

Junior Bear's body

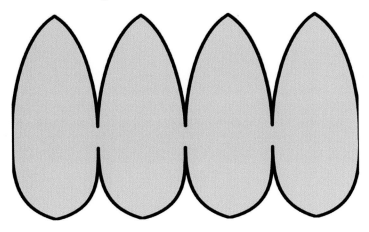

Junior Bear

Junior Bear's job is to help with the chores. Like most youngsters, he sometimes forgets the laundry and gets lost in the fun he can have with a tub full of bubbles.

In this project you'll build a tub using a paper cup as a clay support, and use a garlic press to form the white, sudsy bubbles.

STEP 1   MAKE THE PARTS FOR JUNIOR BEAR

- clay-covered armature: 9" x 12" piece of aluminum foil compressed into a 1" long egg and covered with a ⅛" thick layer of golden tan (Fimo Classic Ochre) clay
- head – ⅞" ball
- ears – ⅜" ball
- nose and eyes – 3mm black beads
- tongue – ⅛" ball
- arms – ⅜" x 3" rope
- legs – ½" x 3" rope
- footpads – ¹⁄₁₆"-thick sheet cut with circle cutters; use the ⅜" cutter for the foot and the ³⁄₁₆" cutter for the toes
- tail – ⅜" ball

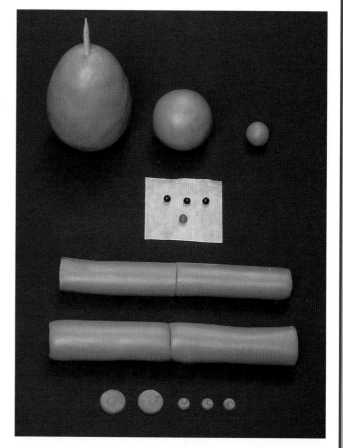

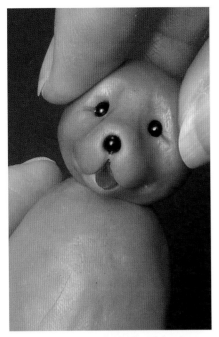

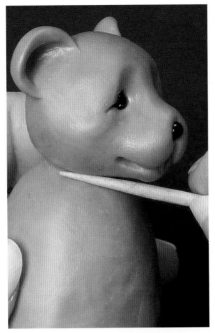

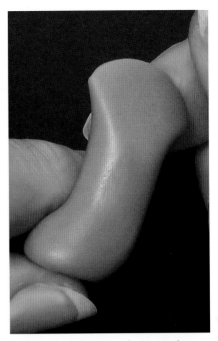

Once you have made the head (as shown in opening section of this chapter) press it down over the exposed toothpick projecting from the body. If the toothpick pushes deeper into the body rather than into the head, pull it out of the body and push it into the head. Then reinsert it into the body. Press and wiggle them together to be certain they stick.

Once the head is securely in position, use a toothpick to roll the seam and smooth the joint.

Legs. Notice there is a change in shape for Junior Bear's leg from that shown earlier. The top has been tapered into a fan-shaped wedge to blend smoothly into his body.

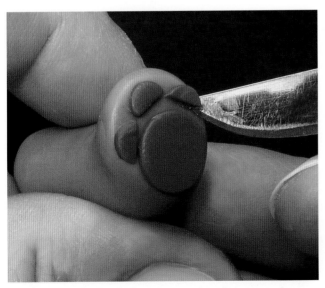

Press the paw pads onto the bottoms of the feet. Toe pads are made by cutting the ³⁄₁₆" circles in half.

Attach the legs and tail. Make and attach the arms.

59

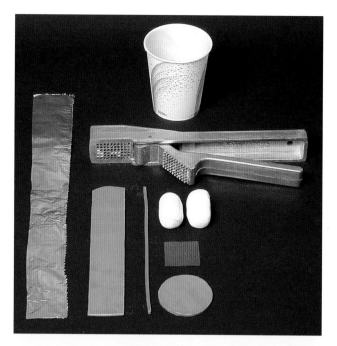

STEP 3 MAKE THE PARTS FOR THE TUB

- 5 oz. paper cup (clay support)
- tub bottom – silver/gray, circle of clay ⅛" thick; use bottom of cup for pattern
- tub sides – silver/gray, ⅛" thick, 1" wide, 6¼" long
- tub top trim – silver/gray, ⅛" thick, ⅛" wide, ⅛" x 6½" long
- bubbles – ¼ block of white clay
- filler – 1½" x 12" piece of foil
- washcloth – ¹⁄₁₆" thick, 1" square of red

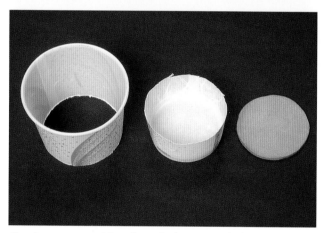

Cut the paper cup 1" up from the bottom and place it on top of the clay circle.

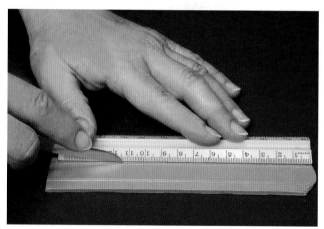

Place the side strip of clay on a piece of waxed paper. Be sure it is straight. Use a ruler and the back of your knife blade to draw two narrow lines ¼" from each edge.

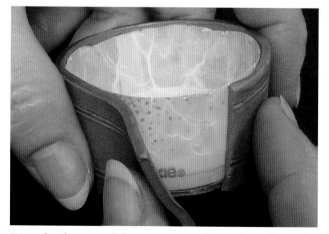

Wrap the clay around the paper cup and press the ends together. Use the back of the knife blade to reestablish the lines on the side of the tub.

Turn the cup bottom up and carefully roll the seam between the side and bottom. Do not press hard or the bottom of the cup will cut through.

Press the top trim on the outside of the cup flush with the top edge. Roll with dowel or brush handle to hide the seam.

STEP 4   THE FIRST BAKE

When the tub is complete, sit Junior next to it and check his arm and leg positions. The tub must be cured before you can remove the paper cup safely (20 minutes at 265° F), and it is best to cure Junior separately because of the longer curing time his head requires (1 hour). You can cure them both in oven at the same time. Place them on separate baking surfaces so the tub can be removed at the end of its time and Junior can continue to bake while you are making the bubbles and wash cloth. Remember, hot clay is extremely fragile! Let the tub cool before you continue working with it. Then remove the paper cup.

STEP 5   MAKE BUBBLES FOR THE TUB

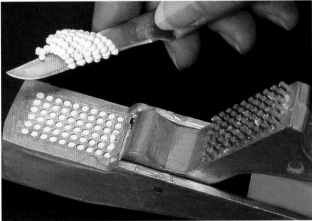

Use the garlic press to make bubbles. Trim the clay at about $\frac{1}{16}"$ x $\frac{1}{8}"$.

Put the crumpled foil strip in the tub and cover it with a generous layer of bubbles. Separate the clay so it isn't in rows.

Fold or wrinkle the wash cloth when it is newly made and still warm and flexible. It may be attached either to the side of the tub or Junior's paws, but not to both. Put the tub with bubbles and the wash cloth into the oven to cure for 20 minutes. Cool and use silver Rub 'n Buff to brighten the outside of the tub if you wish.

Martha Bear (Mama)

Martha knows that being a mother can be a full-time job. Here she is just after baking berry pie.

OPTIONAL BASE

To use a clay base, let the toothpick leg "bone" extend beyond the foot so it can be pushed into the base clay for added support. Even with this support aid, the two pieces of clay must be securely joined.

If you don't use a base, the end of the toothpick should be even with the bottom of the foot. Tricky balancing makes this more difficult for the beginner. It also requires careful bracing during the curing process.

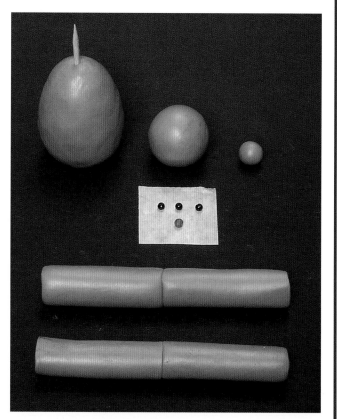

STEP 1 MAKE THE PARTS FOR MAMA BEAR

- clay-covered armature: 12" x 12" piece of aluminum foil compressed into egg 1¾" long and 1½" at thickest area covered with ⅛"-thick layer of golden tan (FIMO Classic Ochre) clay
- head – 1" ball
- ears – ⅜" ball
- nose and eyes – 3mm black beads
- tongue – ⅛" ball
- arms – ½" x 3" rope
- legs – ⅝" x 3½" rope
- tail – ⅜" ball

STEP 2   ASSEMBLE THE BODY, LEGS AND HEAD

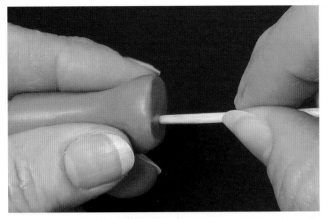

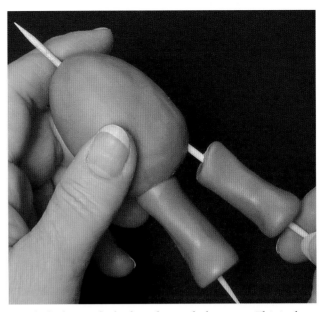

Mama Bear will be standing. To give her more support she will need a simple armature to serve as bones in her legs. To make this, insert a toothpick through the center of each leg. Support the leg from the sides and back as you twist the toothpick into the clay. If you just push and don't support the clay it will compress, throwing off all your measurements.

Attach the legs to the body and smooth the seams. This is also a good time to add the tail. Roll a ⅜" ball and press it on.

Make the head and press it down over the toothpick at the top of the body. Make a rope of clay about 1½" long and taper it at the ends. Use the rope as a neck wrap to fill the space between the head and body to give Mama a thicker neck. Roll and smooth it into place.

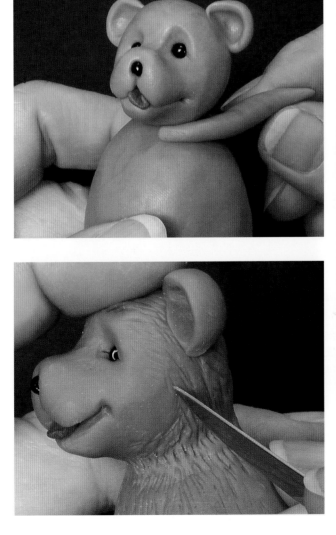

Texture the body and head, but skip the face and ears. Keeping her face smooth helps her look more feminine.

If you elect to stand your bear on a clay base, this is the time to do it. The base should be about ¼" thick. Clip off the tapered part of each toothpick and push them deep into the base. Press each foot securely into place.

STEP 3 MAKE THE FLOWER

Make seven balls smaller than the beads used for the eyes: two green, five white, one yellow. One at a time. flatten each of the green and white balls between your thumb and finger and curl it around the end of a toothpick (like making the tongue) then press it onto the head. Start with the green (leaves). Then the white (petals) and, last, the yellow ball for the center of the flower.

STEP 4 FIRST BAKE

It will take 1 hour at 250° F to cure the head, too long for the thin white apron. The solution is to do a long bake now for the head, body and legs, then a shorter bake (25 minutes) for the apron, arms and pie.

Position Mama so she is balanced and can stand alone before arranging the external bracing to hold her steady during curing. It is important to use bracing during curing whether or not you are using an armature.

To brace for the first bake, put Mama in the same cup arrangement shown for the final bake on page 67. Place the cups close enough that they touch her in four places so she can't shift during baking. Cool her in the oven.

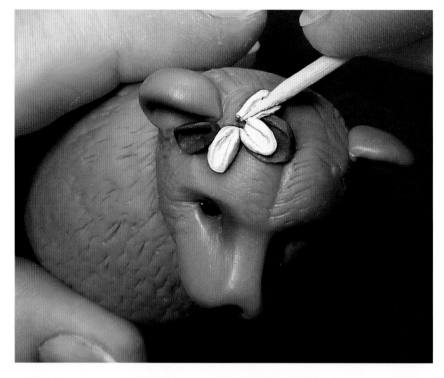

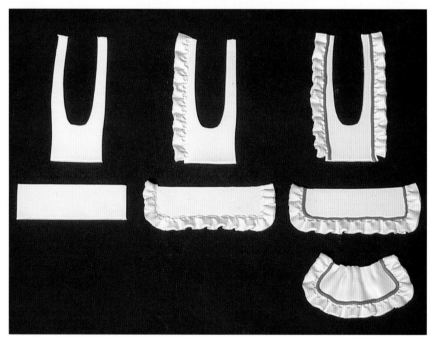

STEP 5 MAKE THE APRON PARTS

- Make one thin sheet of blue clay 1" x 6" and ¹⁄₁₆" thick and one sheet of white clay 4" x 6" and slightly thicker than the blue (#4 on the pasta machine).
- Use the patterns on page 56 to cut out the apron parts.
- Cut several white strips ¼" x 6" that are flat and blunt on the ends.
- Cut several blue strips ¹⁄₁₆" wide for trim.

To make the ruffle, create a series of humps with one of the white strips and a knitting needle. Then use the needle to press and attach each valley.

Next, press the center inside edge of each hump onto the apron with a brush handle. Last, use the end of your tool to press down the end of each new hump.

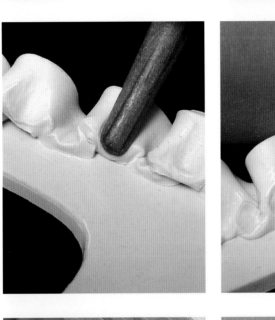

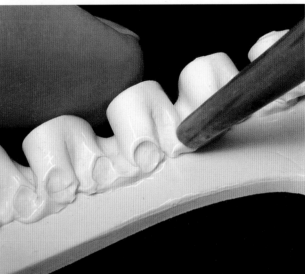

Lay one of the thin blue strips at the very edge of the ruffle to cover irregularities and press with your finger.

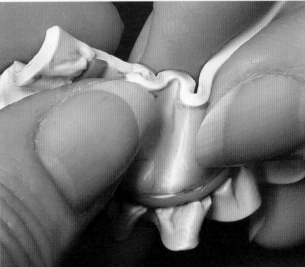

Once the ruffle and trim are attached, gather the skirt edge between your fingers and attach it to Mama's tummy. Trim the top to make a smooth line again.

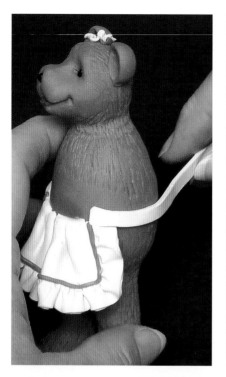

Cut a strip of white a little narrower than a ruffle to use for the belt. Attach the belt even with the blue trim on both sides.

Attach both arms and then the front of the apron. Bring the straps to a V at the belt in the back and trim off any extra.

The bow is a 1" strip the same width as the belt. Fold the ends to the center and press. Turn it on edge and slightly compress the center. Make the ties from two strips of belt.

Use the tip of a brush handle to attach the ties, then the bow, then a tiny ball for the center.

STEP 6   MAKE THE BERRY PIE

- pie pan – bottle cap
- pie filling – ¾" ball of red
- crust – thin sheet of tan (#5 on pasta machine) and paper pattern
- top decoration – three tiny red balls, three tiny green balls

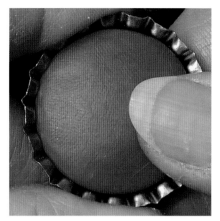

Press the filling into the shell making a smooth dome.

Cut the crust using the paper pattern. Cut slits in the crust and gently stretch over the pie to open the slits. Press the edges with a finger to cut off the surplus and decorate the edge with a knitting needle.

Shape and place the leaves, then add berries. Put the pie between Mama's paws and squeeze them until she can hold it. You may need a tiny drop of instant glue on each paw.

STEP 7   THE FINAL BAKE

The top view of Mama braced between two cups shows she is stabilized in a diamond shape of support. The bowls of the cups will keep her from shifting back or to either side, and the handles keep her from going forward or to either side. The toothpick prop under the pie will prevent it from shifting or making her arms droop during baking, 25 minutes at 250° F.

Bernie Bear (Papa)

Bernie loves tools and gadgets; he's ready to fix things at work or at home. In this project you'll make a toolbelt with gadget-filled pockets, as well as a neat-fitting hat to adorn Papa's head.

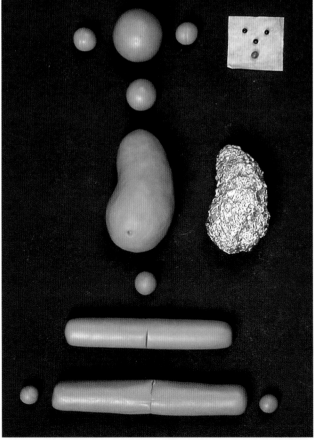

STEP 1 MAKE THE PARTS FOR PAPA

- body – golden tan (FIMO Classic Ochre) clay-covered armature: 12" x 18" piece of aluminum foil compressed into 2½" long egg, 1¼" at thickest area (concave at center front) covered with ⅛" thick layer of clay
- head – 1⅛" ball
- ears – ½" ball (left of head ball in the photo)
- jaw pads – ½" ball (right of head ball)
- tongue – ⅛" red ball
- nose and eyes – 3mm black beads
- neck wrap – ⅝" ball (under head ball)
- arms – ⅝" x 3¾" rope
- tail – ⅜" ball
- legs – ⅝" x 4" rope
- leg wraps – ½" balls

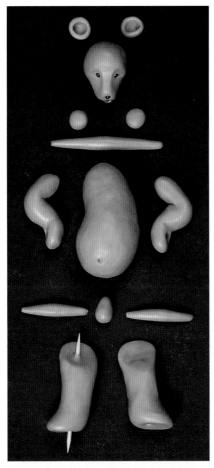

The neck and leg wrap balls should be ropes with tapered ends and the tops of the legs should be fan-shaped wedges with the armature (toothpick) projecting from the inside edge. The paws are slightly stretched and elongated to "droop."

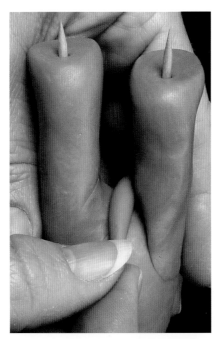

Legs. Attach to the outside bottom of the body, pushing the toothpick into the foil core. Use a leg wrap to fill the gap between the body and the leg.

Head. Attach the head and neck wrap, smoothing the joints before adding the jaw pads. Slightly flatten the ball as you press it into place, and blend the edges into the face.

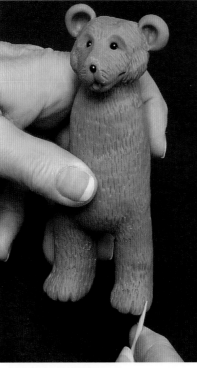

Texture the whole body from head to toe, even the face (except the top and end of his snout and close around his eyes). Ear texturing is optional. Then mark the toe grooves with the side of a toothpick.

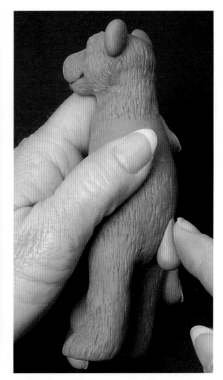

Make the tail ball into a teardrop and press it in place before texturing it.

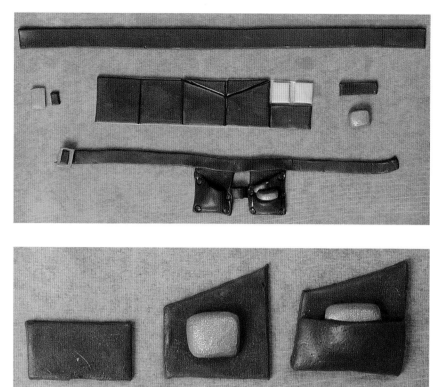

STEP 3 MAKE TOOL BELT

- ¹⁄₁₆" thick rolled sheet of dark brown (FIMO Classic Terra Cotta) clay
- belt – ¼" x 6" (slightly thicker than ¹⁄₁₆")
- buckle – thin roll of silver or gray clay cut same width as belt with tiny overlay of dark brown
- pockets – cut five squares ⅝" wide from ¹⁄₁₆" thick strip: two plain, two angled at the top edge, one cut in half
- strap between pockets – ³⁄₁₆" x ⅝" (cut from same ¹⁄₁₆" strip as pockets)
- tape measure – ⅛" thick, ¼" square, silver or gray
- pocket fillers – shown in yellow ¹⁄₁₆" thick, ¼" square

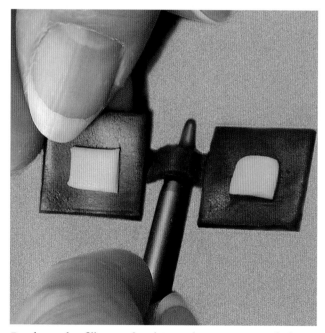

Place the "tape measure" on top of an angled square of brown and cover part of it with the half pocket.

Put the pocket fillers on the plain pocket squares. Attach the pocket squares to the strap that fits between them and move them close enough to create a hump in the strap.

Put the angled pockets over the plain pockets, covering the pocket fillers, and press the sides and bottoms together. *Do not* press the top angled edge down. Use the back of your knife blade to mark a line on both long edges of the belt. Center the side of the belt over the top edges of the plain pockets and join them. Use the hollow end of an retractable ballpoint pen to make marks where rivets would be.

Attach the tool belt to Papa, angling the sides to make it higher in the back. Trim the ends of the belt so they meet in the center of the back and cover the joint with the belt buckle.

STEP 4 FIRST BAKE
It is important to use external bracing while curing. You can do this in two ways—by propping things against your project or strapping it to a support with a strip of waxed paper and a paperclip. Bake Papa for 1 hour at 265° F and cool him in the oven.

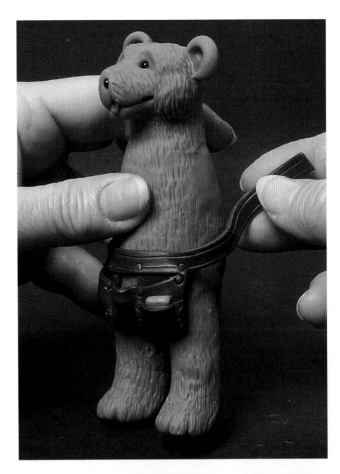

Balance Papa so he can stand alone. Then brace him for baking. Bracing with cups provides four points of contact to keep him from shifting in any direction.

Another bracing technique would be strapping him to a support with a waxed paper strip to keep him from shifting.

DOES POLYMER CLAY FADE IN THE SUN?
Yes. Colors will fade when exposed to the rays of the sun for extended periods.

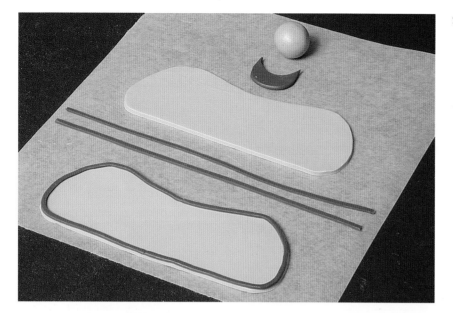

STEP 5 MAKING HAT AND VEST

- vest – ¹⁄₁₆" sheet of light blue clay and the paper pattern
- trim – two ¹⁄₁₆" strips of dark blue for trim
- hat – ⅝" ball of light blue and thin sheet of dark blue (slightly thicker than jacket trim), and paper pattern for hat bill

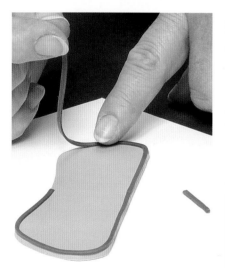

Cut out the vest and carefully trim the edge with a strip of dark blue. The side with the curve in it is the top of the vest.

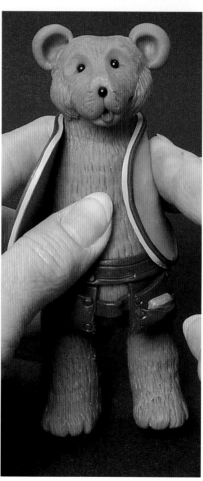

Put the center of the vest top at the center of the neck. Wrap the vest to the front and position it before you start pressing to attach it.

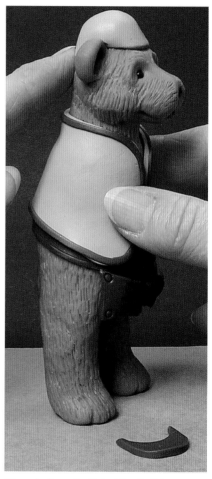

Next, hollow the light blue ball into a cup using a rounded dowel or large brush handle. Turn the cup upside down and attach it to Papa's head.

Press the hat bill into the grove between the hat and the head.

Use the back of your knife blade to mark the lines in the hat.

Attach the arms, retexture if necessary, and place a thin strip of trim around the upper arm-vest seam to finish the vest. Brace Papa, give him a final bake of 40 minutes at 250° F, let him cool, and he is finished.

Benny Bear (Baby)

Benny is a tiny little bear like the animals in chapter three (no armature), but that's the way babies are. The only extra accessory for him is a bow made from a small strip of clay—use whatever color you like best.

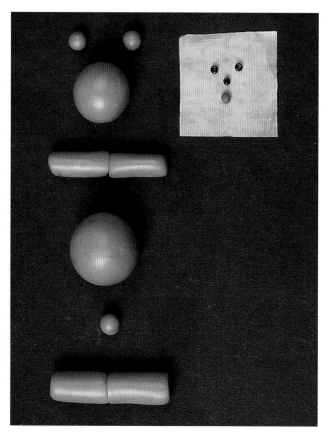

STEP 1   MAKE THE PARTS FOR BABY

- ears – two ¼" golden tan (FIMO Classic Ochre) balls
- head – ¾" ball
- eyes and nose – black seed beads
- tongue – tiny red ball, a little bigger than a seed bead
- arms – ¼" x 1½" rope
- body – ⅞" ball
- tail – ¼" ball
- legs – ⅜" x 1½" rope

STEP 2   ASSEMBLE AND TEXTURE BABY

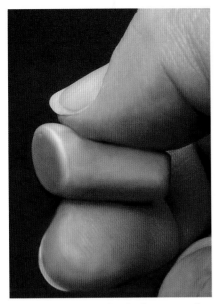

Join the body, legs and head. Texture from the head down (working in rows around the body will help maintain the shape). Texture and attach the arms as you work. Stop after both arms are attached to make and attach the bow.

After pressing to make the foot it may be necessary to roll the leg between your finger and thumb to re-establish its shape. Using an internal support for the leg is optional with this little fellow.

STEP 3   MAKE THE BOW

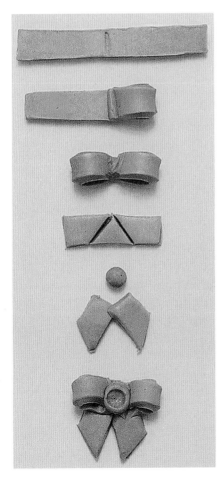

Make the bow using a ¹⁄₁₆" strip of light blue clay, ⅛" wide. Trim a piece 1" long, loop the ends back to the center and attach. Flip the bow on edge and slightly compress the center joint with the side of a toothpick. Repeat on the other side.

Cut the ½" ties from the same strip. Cut a triangular notch at the center. Roll the clay from the notch into a ball that will form the knot at the center of the bow. Turn the blunt ends of the remaining pieces toward each other and join two corners.

Place the bow over the blunt ends of the ties and press the ball from the notch onto the center of the bow using the end of a brush handle.

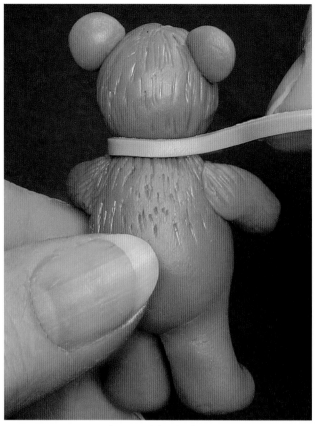

Cut a strip narrower than used for the bow and wrap it around Benny's neck, covering the grove between his head and body. Start and end under his chin so the bow will cover the seam.

Lift the finished bow with your knife and slide into position. Attach by pressing the knot again with a brush handle.

STEP 4   TEXTURE AND BAKE

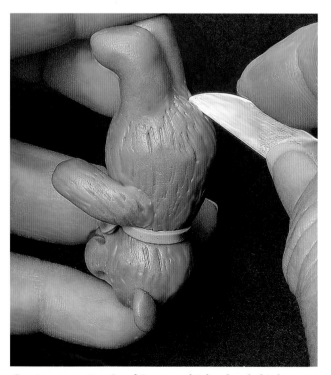

Before texturing the tops of his feet, straighten and position Benny so he will balance and can stand. Now, texture, brace and bake for 45 minutes at 250° F.

Continue texturing. Stand Benny on his head to do his lower body. Then add his tail.

Simple variations and combining techniques from other projects will add to your bear family possibilities.

Simple variations allow you to embellish, stabilize or just add variety to what you can do. For example, you can have Junior Bear both smooth and textured, Mama Bear freestanding and with a clay base, Baby Bear both standing and seated, with and without a flower behind the ear and with different colors of bows to indicate boy or girl. Another thing you can do is put miniature (dollhouse) accessories with your projects, such as Papa's tools and toolbox. You could buy Mama's pie or Junior's tub already made. There are many ready-made accessories available in the miniature section of hobby and craft stores.

CHAPTER FIVE

Advanced Projects

The more advanced your clay projects become, the more you will need to refine their armatures and surface treatments. A crushed foil armature can be shaped to provide a more complex base than the simple egg used with the bears. A shaped foil core will require a bit more time but it will help avoid thick areas of clay that require prolonged baking and cooling times. Also, the simple toothpick used in the bear legs will be replaced with shaped wire to provide not only greater strength, but also more stability. In this chapter you will refine armature shapes, work toward a more consistent clay thickness in your finished projects, learn intricate surface detailing, and create more complex costumes and props.

I USED THESE COLORS

FIMO Soft: White, Nightglow, Lemon Yellow, Sunflower, Indian Red, Windsor Blue, Terra Cotta, Tropical Green, Plum, Caramel, Sahara, Fluorescent Blue, Chocolate, Black, Metallic Gold, Metallic Silver, and FIMO Stone Color Jasper

---

WHAT YOU'LL NEED

Clay (generic color names)
• yellow, tan, medium brown, dark brown, white, navy blue, black, gold, brown (with fibers), turquoise blue, red, green purple, and glow-in-the-dark silver or gray

Cutting tools
• Kemper circle cutters:
  ³⁄₁₆" (PC5R)
  ³⁄₈" (PC3R)
  ¾" (PCBR)
• four-leaf cutter (AMACO Friendly Cutter set #5)
• sharp craft knife
• one dull, thin-bladed paring knife
• single-edge razor blade, NuBlade (AMACO) or Tissue Slicing Blade (Kemper)

Other clay tools
• cutting and measuring template for polymer clay or ruler
• rolling pin or pasta machine

Paints and brushes
• acrylic paint, dark gray or black
• no. 3 round and no. 7 round paint brushes
• dark gray powder eyeshadow
• powder rouge or rose/rust eyeshadow

Miscellaneous
• AMACO Double-Ended Clay Shaper (TPCR #2)
• 7"length of a ¼" wooden dowel with rounded end or brush handle
• 3mm black beads
• round toothpicks
• knitting needle
• two standard (#1) paperclips
• aluminum foil
• waxed paper
• tracing paper or typing paper
• wire cutters
• 14-gauge wire or a lightweight clothes hanger
• pliers

Shelby Navy Seal

Shelby Seal is a Navy man. His foil core and wire foot armature is simple and made with supplies found in most homes. The armature will allow him to stand safely on his own two feet—or should I say flippers—even before the clay is added. His tidy uniform is assembled from simple sheets of white clay (with navy blue trim); the patterns on the opposite page will help you out.

> **I USED THESE COLORS**
> FIMO Soft: Chocolate, Black, White and Windsor Blue

STEP 1   MAKE THE PARTS FOR SHELBY

- clay-covered armature – 12" x 18" piece of aluminum foil, 5" long and 1" at thickest area, covered with 3" x 5" rectangle of brown clay ⅛" thick (pattern A)
- paperclips to make wire armature for flippers
- eyes – 3mm black beads
- nose – triangle with ⅛" sides cut from 1⁄16" thick black sheet of clay or a 3mm black bead
- arms/flippers – cut from ⅛" thick sheet of brown clay (patterns E, F, G)
- feet/flippers bottom – cut from ⅛" thick sheet of brown clay (pattern G)
- feet/flippers top – ⅝" ball of brown, roll to 1½" rope tapered at both ends, cut at center

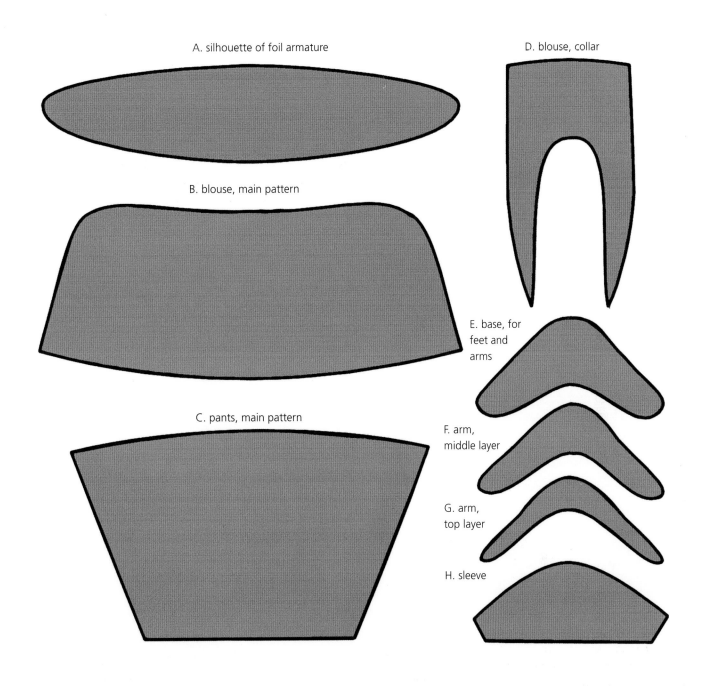

A. silhouette of foil armature

D. blouse, collar

B. blouse, main pattern

C. pants, main pattern

E. base, for feet and arms

F. arm, middle layer

G. arm, top layer

H. sleeve

STEP 2   MAKE SHELBY'S CLOTHING

- hat crown – ½" white ball
- hat brim – ¼" x 3½" cut from a ¹⁄₁₆" thick white sheet; this same sheet of clay can be used to make the pants cuff (³⁄₁₆" x 3½")
- navy blue trim – ¹⁄₁₆" x 2", ¹⁄₁₆" thick
- navy blue ties – ³⁄₁₆" x 2", slightly more than ¹⁄₁₆" thick
- optional piece at throat, under blouse and collar – white triangle ³⁄₈" sides
- tie keeper – ⅛" x ½", slightly more than ¹⁄₁₆" thick
- blouse and blue trim and pants are made from sheets of white and navy blue clay ¹⁄₁₆" thick
- pants cuff – ³⁄₁₆" x 3½", ¹⁄₁₆" thick; trim to length once in place

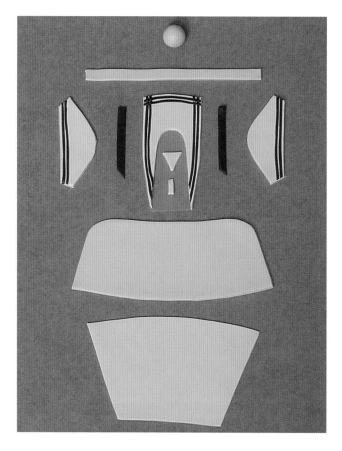

STEP 3   ASSEMBLE THE BODY

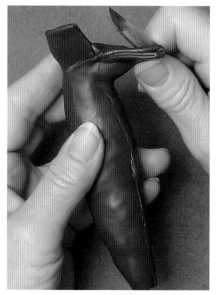

Make a shape 5" long and 1" wide at the center. Taper the ends, but allow the center to remain full. Bend 1" from the end to make the head. Compress the front and sides of the neck narrower than the head. Use a dowel or brush handle to press in shallow eye sockets. The eyes should be about halfway between the back of the head and the nose tip. Cover the foil with a clay shell ⅛" thick.

Wrap the clay sheet from the back to the front. Work the clay onto the surface by gently pressing from the center of the sheet toward the edges as you cover the foil armature. To trim away excess clay, overlap the extra and cut through both layers. Remove any double thickness of clay above or below the cut before compressing and smoothing the seam.

As the clay is pressed onto the armature you will get a fin or fold of extra clay sticking out of the sculpture. Press the base of the fold to fit the clay to the armature then cut the fin off and smooth the seam.

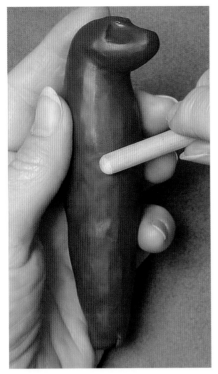

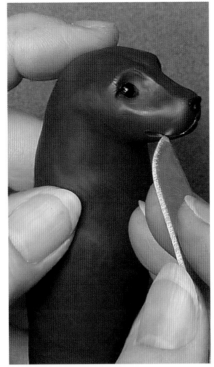

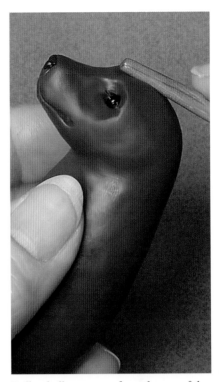

Roll and refine the surface starting at the head to work air bubbles down and out the open end of the body. Trim and seal the end.

Head. Use the rounded end of the dowel to refine the nose and eye area. Add the bead eyes and nose triangle. The mouth is a shallow cut. Press in nostrils and round the corners of the mouth with the end of a knitting needle.

Roll a shallow groove from the top of the head to the top of the nose (between the eyes) to separate the eye ridges.

Tail. The armature for the tail flippers is made with two 1" paperclips. Use a pair of pliers to straighten the large outside loops of the clips and bend them 90°. Push the straightened wires up into the body. Put the clay flipper base on waxed paper, position the body toward the back and center the small loops of the paper clips on the clay base. Push the foot ropes into place by pressing at an angle along the sides so you don't flatten the foot. The wide ends of the foot ropes hold the body securely in place and the narrow end tapers all the way to the toe. Now balance Shelby so he can stand.

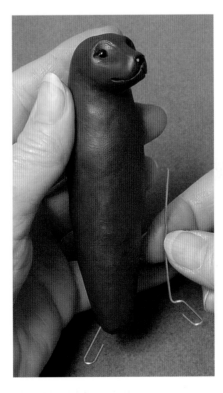

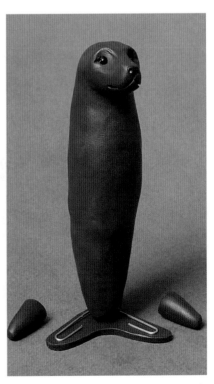

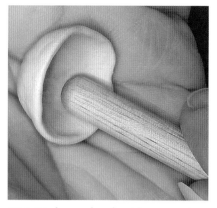

Hat. Wash your hands with soap and dry them on a white towel to keep your white clay clean. Use the rounded end of your dowel to hollow the ¼" ball to make the hat crown.

Add the hat brim.

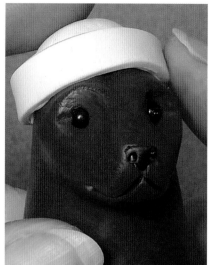

Attach the hat to his head and adjust the shape of the crown and angles of the brim.

STEP 4   FIRST BAKE

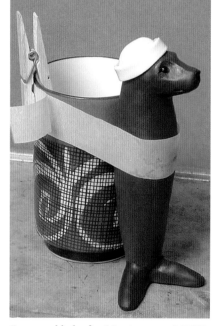

Brace and bake for 20 minutes at 265° F.

STEP 5   ASSEMBLE THE UNIFORM

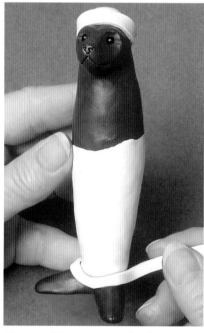

The top of the pants is wider than the bottom. Attach one edge of pants to the center of the back and work around the body. Repeat for the cuff. The cuff can be made from the same sheet of clay as the hat brim, ³⁄₁₆" x 3". Blend the top of the pants into the body so there is a smooth transition. Any irregularities will show through the shirt.

Center the blouse on Shelby's back and wrap both sides to the front. Do not overlap the edges. Trim, compress or gently stretch to make it fit smoothly.

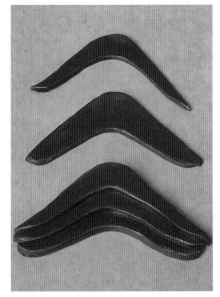

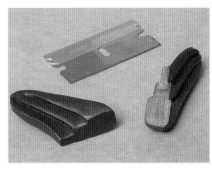

Smooth and round the thick top edge of this stack, then cut it in half with a sharp blade like a razor blade, a tissue blade, or a NuBlade. The sharper and thinner the blade, the less distortion to your clay shape.

Arm flippers. There are five arm/flipper pieces. The largest is the center of the flipper sandwiched between the two medium pieces that are topped by the two smallest pieces.

Wrap each flipper with a sleeve and attach it to the seal.

Cross the necktie pieces and squeeze the center to join and make a groove for the white tie wrap. Wrap the white tie band around the groove and press it onto the blouse front. Secure the long upper ends of the ties onto the shoulders.

Center the collar at the back of the neck and join in a V just above the ties. Trim the ends if necessary to make a smooth joint between the blouse and collar.

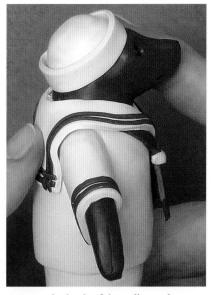

Arrange the back of the collar and curve the arms slightly to the front.

STEP 6   THE FINAL BAKE

Make a four-point brace with two cups for the last bake. Bake for 30 minutes at 250° F and cool in the oven.

Judge Owlbert

Judge Owlbert is fastidious about details and believes in having everything in its proper place. The tasks he presents us with are not difficult, only time consuming—and there are some short cuts to accomplishing them! He is kind enough to require only a simple armature, very similar to the ones used earlier for the bears, so you can concentrate on surface detailing.

> **I USED THESE COLORS**
> FIMO Soft: White, Sunflower, Black, Chocolate, Sahara, Caramel and Gold

STEP 1   MAKE THE PARTS FOR OWLBERT

- eye (upper left) – pattern L, plus ½" black circle, ⅜" yellow circle, and ½" black circle (all ⅟₁₆" thick)
- horn feathers (upper right) – three layers of clay slightly more than ⅟₁₆" thick (patterns B and K)
- bill – ⅜" yellow ball
- clay-covered shaped armature – 12" x 18" foil crushed to 1½" x ½" (see pattern G); cover with ⅛" layer of clay
- breast feathers, white and tan; body feathers, white, medium brown and dark brown (layers of clay ⅟₁₆" or less thick) – cut with the four-leaf pattern cutter from Friendly Cutters Set #5 (or use pattern M)
- wings, wing wedges, and tail – ⅛" thick sheets of tan and dark brown (patterns C, H and J)
- legs – ¾" balls of medium brown (made into 1" cones)
- feet/toes – ¼" x 3" yellow rope marked at ½" intervals to cut for toes

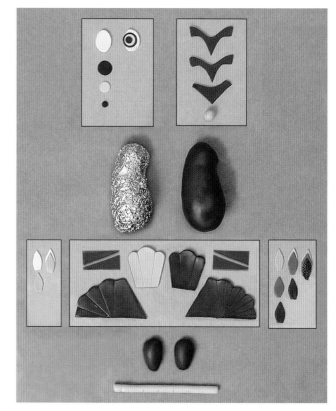

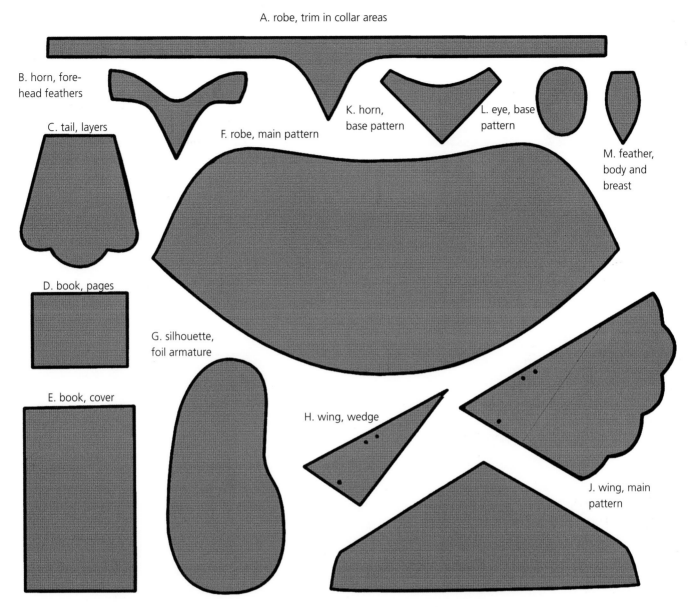

A. robe, trim in collar areas

B. horn, fore-head feathers

C. tail, layers

F. robe, main pattern

K. horn, base pattern

L. eye, base pattern

M. feather, body and breast

D. book, pages

G. silhouette, foil armature

E. book, cover

H. wing, wedge

J. wing, main pattern

I. robe, sleeve

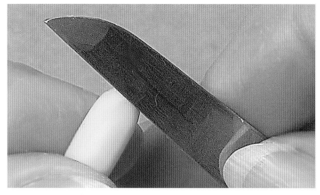

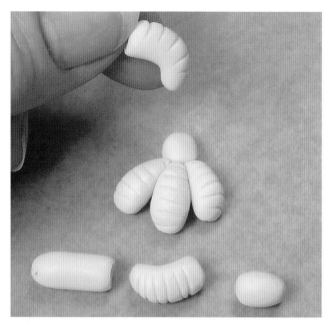

Feet. Cut the foot rope into six pieces ½" long and two pieces ¼" long. Round the ends and curl the short rope over the end of your finger to form a hooked toe. Roll the back of your knife blade over the toe several times to create a bird toe texture.

Group three of the long toes and pinch the blunt ends together. Add one of the short toes to the back and join the foot to the narrow end of a leg cone.

Attach the legs to the body.

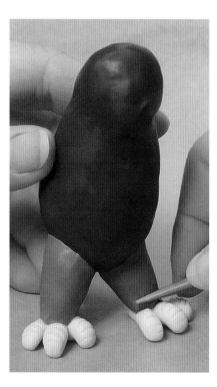

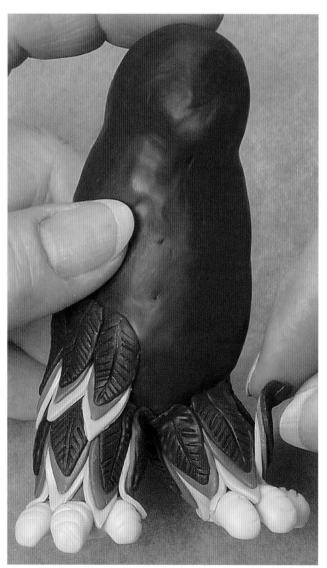

Feathering. Feather the legs first. (See the following page for how to make feathers.) The tips of the first row of feathers will slightly overlap the foot. The clay cone of the leg will show slightly between the tips. The top half of the feathers will touch, hiding the leg cones and body's clay shell. The second row of feathers will be on the lower body, but will overlap the leg enough to hide where those feathers blend into the leg. The first breast feather will be used in this row, low on the tummy and between the top of the legs. The tail will be attached before application of the third row of feathers.

HOW TO MAKE FEATHERS

If you have a pasta machine and the four-leaf cutter from AMACO's Friendly Cutter set #5, your feather making will be much simpler. You need thin sheets of clay in white, tan and dark brown (use setting #5 to make your clay slightly less than 1⁄16" thick). Place each sheet of clay on a separate piece of waxed paper. If you do not have a four-leaf cutter, trace the paper pattern M.

Place clay sheets on waxed paper. Use the four-leaf cutter. Place the cutter at the side of your clay sheet and cut.

To remove feathers from the cutter, place a tool through the center opening and lift the end of the clay. Place the feather on a sheet of waxed paper to ensure easy handling later.

Body feathers are made by layering three feather colors together. Each color is slightly offset, allowing the tip of the lower colors to show; the top remains thin where it will attach to the body. The breast feathers have only two layers, also offset. Texture by making a line down the center of each feather and then marking both sides with the back of your knife blade.

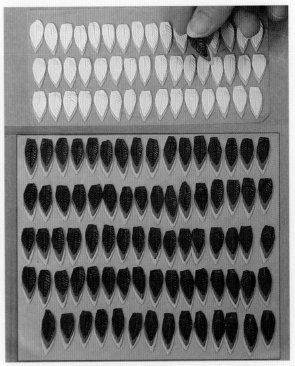

Prepare to make a lot of layered and textured feathers. You will need 18 breast feathers and 58 body feathers.

Tail. The tail is made of two offset layers of clay. The feather markings are pressed or drawn into the surface with the back of a knife blade. The top layer of dark brown is textured on only one surface. The bottom layer of tan is textured on the bottom surface and the lower edge of the top surface. They may be textured before or after they are joined together, but should be textured before being attached to the body.

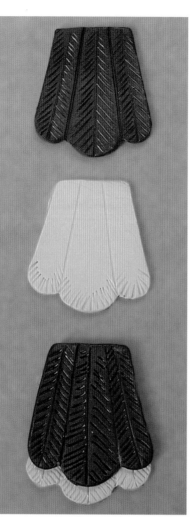

Attach the tail to the body in such a way that it will serve as a third support to help Owlbert stand. The weight should be on the legs and feet—the tail is to stabilize only.

Three body feathers are used to fill the crack under the tail and help stabilize it. You may need to trim a bit off the blunt ends of the feather so they don't cover too much of the tail.

The third row of feathers uses only three breast feathers on the lower tummy. The fourth and fifth rows have four light and two dark feathers on the front of the body. That is all that will show once the robe is in place. The sixth row will circle the neck. Narrow to three breast feathers in front, and use body feathers on the sides and back. The bill will be centered above the breast feathers so it touches the end of the center feather. The body feathers should be about ¼" higher on the head than the breast feathers, arching slightly toward the back. Notice that the armature's clay shell has feather marks pressed into the areas between the points of the feathers to be sure any area above the robe will look feathered.

One more row of body feathers should cover the top of the head.

Attach the bill and make nostrils with a sharpened dowel or tip of a knitting needle. Use the cut feathers around the bottom of the bill. Attach both ends but let the center of each curve puff a little.

Face. Assemble the eyes, shape the bill and mark the beak's separation. Shorten the blunt ends of three breast feathers making crescent-shaped cuts.

Attach the eyes at an angle, close together but not touching at the top. The outside of each eye should stand away from the side of the head, leaving a small gap.

Horn feathers. The center point of the first layer of horn feathers is attached to the bill first, then arched over each eye and attached to the head just behind the white of the eye. Press the back edge of the shape onto the head, but be careful not to flatten the front of the arch down over the eye.

The second and third layers of horn feathers are attached in the center first, then along the center two-thirds of the back edge. The ends must remain free so they can be curled up to make the horns. Each layer is offset to give the horns a larger shape and more dramatic effect.

STEP 3   FIRST BAKE

Check Owlbert's posture and balance before bracing and baking.

Create a four-point brace so he can't shift, then bake for 40 minutes at 250° F.

STEP 4   MAKE THE BOOK

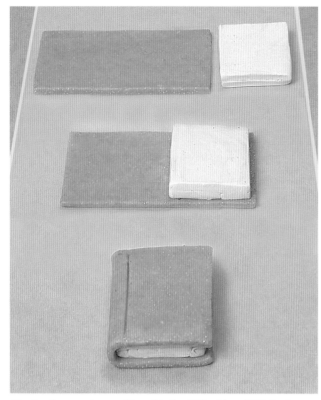

The book cover is metallic gold clay 1⅛" x 2" and ⅟₁₆" thick. The white pages are ¾" x 1" and ⅛" thick. Use patterns D and E. The crease marking the spine of the book is pressed with the back of a knife blade. Crease both sides.

STEP 5   MAKE THE ROBE

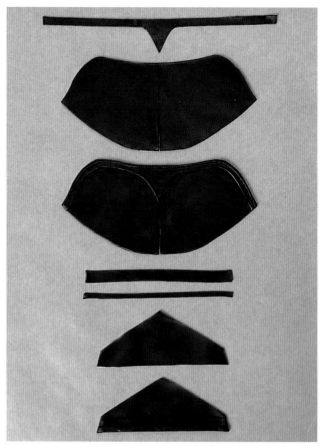

The robe and sleeves are made from a sheet of black ⅟₁₆" thick. Place the clay sheet on waxed paper for easier handling. Use paper patterns F and I for size and shape. The trim pieces are thinner. The sleeve trim is two bands, one ¼" wide and the other ⅛" wide. The photograph shows the robe, sleeves and trim as separate pieces and then layered together. Additional detailing can be drawn into the trim.

Center the robe on the back and gently but firmly press into place. The front of the robe is to be open and overlaps only part of the outer feathers. Do not press the front edges of the robe flat against the breast.

STEP 6 MAKE THE WINGS

Cut and assemble the wings. Draw the feather markings with the back of a knife blade. Sandwich the top of the wing between two wing wedges and round the top edge.

Wrap the sleeve around the wing and join it at the bottom.

STEP 7 ATTACH THE WINGS AND BOOK, FINAL BAKE

Attach the wings to the body. Cradle the book in the wing but not tight against the chest. Hold the book in place by pressing it against the elbow between the wing and front of the robe. Gently pinch to stick the wing, book and robe together. Brace and bake for 35 minutes at 250° F. Cool in the oven.

Kerri Kangaroo, Artist

Complex body shapes and skinny legs require special armatures. For this project, you will use a segmented foil core and 14-gauge wire. You will also use one of the clays with a fiber in it that adds visual texture and physical strength to delicate projections and thin areas of clay. The clay used for the main portion of this project is FIMO Stone Jasper. You will notice that the clay retains its visual texture even when mixed with other non-fiber clay.

> **I USED THESE COLORS**
> FIMO Soft: Jasper, Sahara, Black, White, Sunflower, Indian Red, Plum, Flourescent Blue, Tropical Green and Pacific Blue

STEP 1   MAKE THE ARMATURE PIECES

- body – 12" x 18" foil crushed to fit body pattern A. Notice the curved indentation to form the back of the jaw and the slight upward curve to the nose.
- tail – 4" x 6" foil crushed to 1¼" long cone, blunt at both ends, one end ¾" wide and the other ⅜" wide. Press the tail rope against the lower back of the body to insure a smooth fit. Use 14-gauge wire in the legs (4") and arms (1"). You will need pliers to bend the wires.

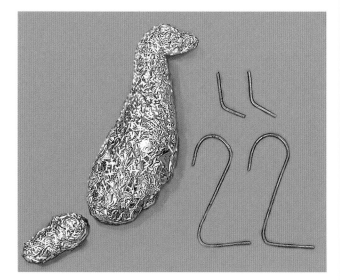

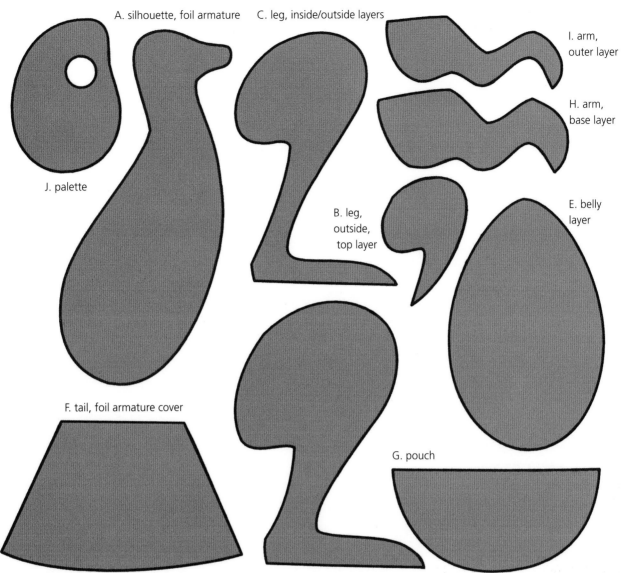

A. silhouette, foil armature

C. leg, inside/outside layers

I. arm, outer layer

H. arm, base layer

J. palette

B. leg, outside, top layer

E. belly layer

F. tail, foil armature cover

G. pouch

D. leg, base layer

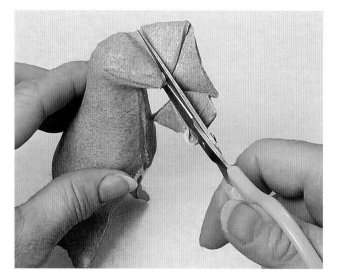

STEP 2   COVER THE BODY

Cover the body with a ⅛" thick shell of clay that is a 50/50 blend of FIMO Stone Jasper (with fibers) and Sahara (light tan). Start with a 4" x 6" rectangle wrapping from the back to the front. Trim or fill as necessary. Roll and smooth surface.

STEP 3   MAKE PARTS FOR KERRI

- colors: light pieces, 50/50 brown with fibers (FIMO Soft Jasper) and white (no fibers); darker pieces same as the original body shell (Jasper plus Sahara)
- stomach – (left) light egg shape, 1/16" thick (pattern E)
- pouch – light semi-circle, ⅛" thick (pattern G)
- ears – (center top) 1/16" thick; dark circle is ¾"; light circle is ⅝", slightly thinner than #5 on the pasta machine
- eyelids – crescents 1/16" thick, cut using a ⅜" circle cutter
- eyes – black 3mm beads
- snout – ¼" ball cut in half
- tail – (bottom center) ⅛" thick, used to wrap the foil tail cone (pattern J)
- tail end – 1" ball of clay formed into tapered rope 3½" long, ½" diameter and blunt at the widest end

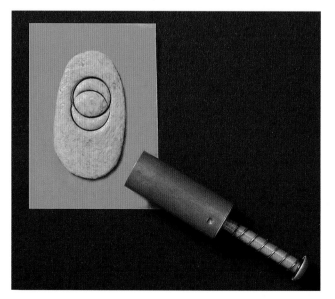

The eyelid crescents are made by overlapping two circle cuts. Place your clay on waxed paper, cut, and remove extra clay. Lift each crescent with knife and position it on the head.

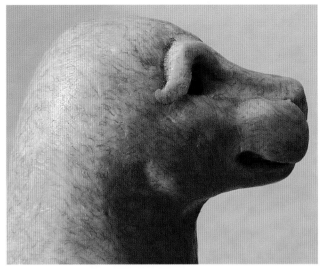

Head. The head has been rolled and smoothed. The jaw curve is reestablished using the side and tapered end of a knitting needle or small brush handle. The bead eyes (smooth side to front) are set into the head before the eyelids are attached and blended into place. Cut ¼" ball in half and press onto the sides of the muzzle to form the upper lip. Indicate the sides of the nose/nostril area and blend into place. Cut the mouth and round the corners.

Refine the nose by rolling with the rounded end of a dowel or brush handle. Add the nostrils. A toothpick can be used to help define the lower outside curves of the nose.

Tail. Wrap the clay shell around the tail armature.

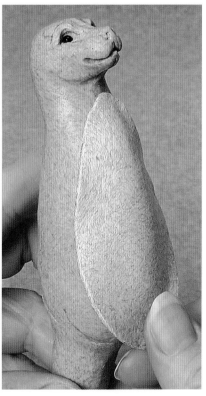

Join the two sections of tail.

Join the tail to the body. Attach the light stomach patch and blend the edges into the darker body. Be careful to press out any air trapped under the clay.

The back legs are constructed in layers. Each leg requires four carefully cut ⅛" thick pieces: patterns D, C and B.

To make the leg, center a leg wire on the largest dark leg shape.

Cover the wire with a light leg shape, matching the bottom edges of the foot and centering the remainder of the leg. Press the middle and heel of the foot together, but not the toes.

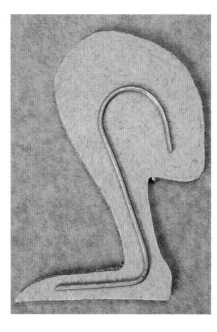

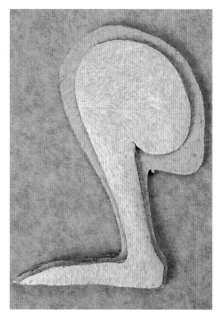

Turn the leg over and layer the two remaining leg pieces onto the original leg.

Blend the pieces, rounding and smoothing the top of the upper leg, but retaining some of the layered look in the lower leg to show tendons. Repeat the process with the foot pointed in the other direction for the other leg.

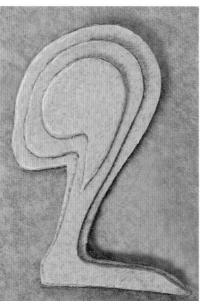

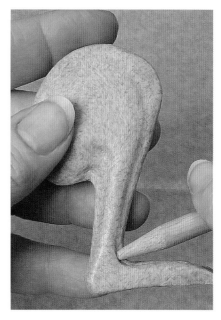

Join the legs to the body and adjust until Kerri stands.

STEP 6   MAKE THE EARS

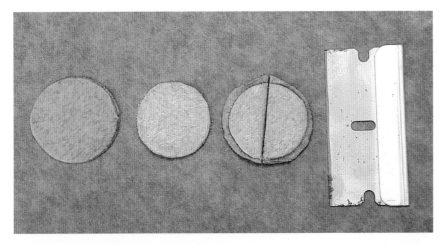

Center the light circle on top of the dark one, press together and cut in half with a sharp blade. A single downward push works better than pulling the blade for this cut.

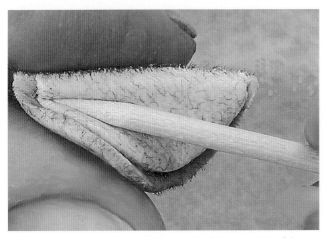

To make the tip of the ear, curl one end of the cut side of the circle part of the way around a toothpick.

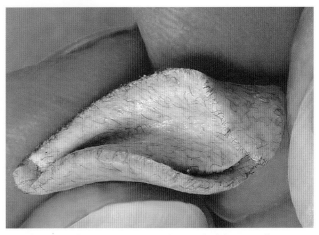

For the base of the ear, curl the other end of the cut edge to form a cone. The curl starts about ¼" from the point (on the rounded edge of the circle). The point of the cut edge will be joined to the curved outside of the circle so the flat edge forms the top of the cone.

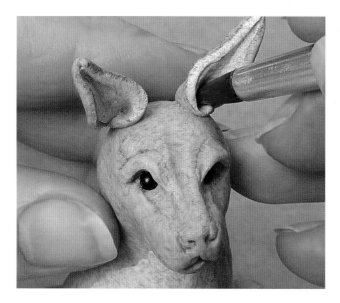

Join the ear to the head using the cone-shaped end of a Double-Ended Clay Shaper. The flexible rubber tip responds much like a tiny soft finger. A knitting needle or tapered dowel will also work. Blend the back of the ear to cover the seam.

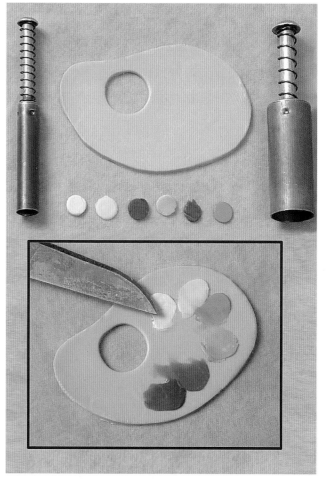

STEP 7   FIRST BAKE

It is now time to position, brace and bake in a preheated oven at 250° F for 40 minutes. Use a four-point bracing system like the bear projects so the legs and body won't shift. While baking and cooling, make Kerri's paint supplies.

STEP 8   MAKE THE ACCESSORIES

Cut the paint palette from a thin sheet of light tan clay using the pattern. Make the thumbhole with a ⅜" circle cutter. The circles of paint are made with the ³⁄₁₆" circle cutter and smeared with the side of a knife blade after placement on the palette. The pieces are cut from ¹⁄₁₆" thick sheets of clay. The paint palette should be baked on a flat surface before it is fitted into the hand.

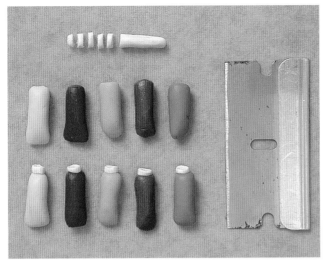

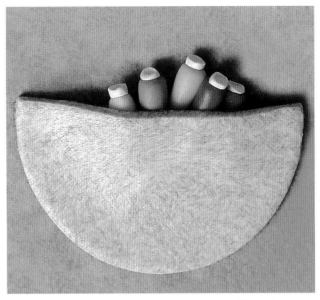

The paint tubes are ropes ³⁄₁₆" in diameter and ½" long. The bottom end of each is flattened slightly. The caps for the paint tubes are sliced from a tiny white rope and pressed on using the end of a small brush handle or tapered dowel. Use a sharp blade when cutting to avoid crushing the rope.

Arrange the paint tubes. Cover the lower part of the tubes with the pouch and press gently to stick them all together. Be sure to leave room for the paint cloth.

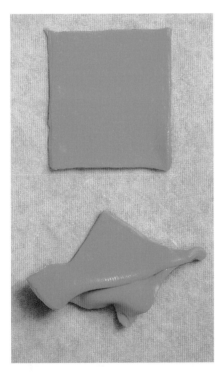

The paint cloth measures 1" x 1¼" x ¹⁄₁₆" thick and is wrinkled diagonally. Only one corner is tucked into the pouch. The cloth can be put in the pocket either before or after it is attached to the body.

STEP 9 ATTACH THE POUCH

Tuck the sides of the pouch deep into the crevice between the leg and body, pressing and blending the edges with a tool if your finger doesn't fit. The pouch will not reach clear to the lower edge of the stomach patch. Fold the paint cloth down over the edge of the pouch after it is attached to the body.

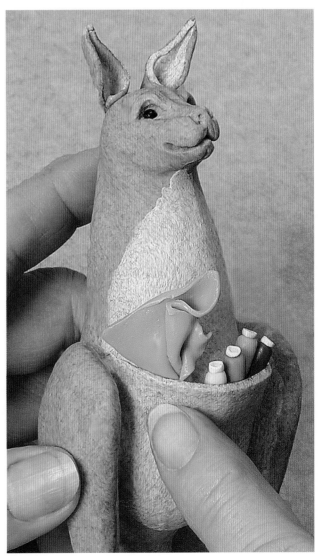

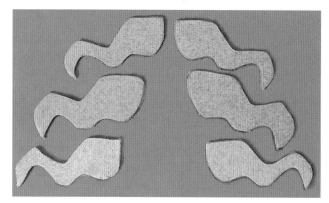

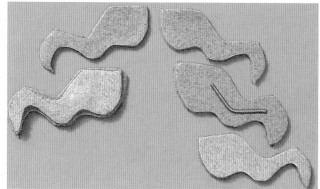

Each arm is composed of three layers; each is ⅛" thick. Locate the wire between the light inside layer and the larger of the brown pieces. The smaller arm pieces should be centered on the larger central piece as you did with the back leg. Do not press the toes/fingers together.

WHAT KIND OF GLUE DO YOU RECOMMEND FOR POLYMER CLAY?

Silicone glues such as Goop or E-6000 are good for larger objects and to attach cured clay items to metal or wood. Super Glue Gel or Zap A Gap can be used to glue metal findings to cured clay or to mend broken pieces. Deco Cement is slow setting glue that works well. Flexible types of hot melt glues can be used, but are not on my preferred list of ways to join clay pieces.

Sculpey Diluent (softening agent) is very useful as an adhesive for attaching *uncured* pieces. Put Diluent on one side, attach to other piece, and then cure. The plasticizer in the diluent creates an incredibly strong bond.

White craft glues like Tacky Glue or Elmer's Glue tend to pop off the clay because they are not flexible.

Attach the front legs/arms.

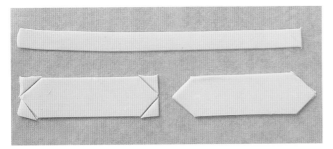

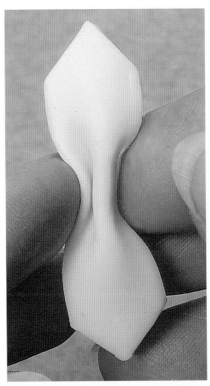

Ascot. The ascot (neck scarf) is made of two pieces of clay. The neckband is ¼" wide and 3½" long. The tie is ½" wide and 1¾" long. They are ⅟₁₆" thick.

Trim the ends of the tie to make points and compress the center. Press it onto one end of the neckband so it forms a T. Do not fold the tie over the neckband until after it is in place around the neck and trimmed to fit. A tiny drop of instant glue on the back of the neckband/tie joint will help stick it to the body.

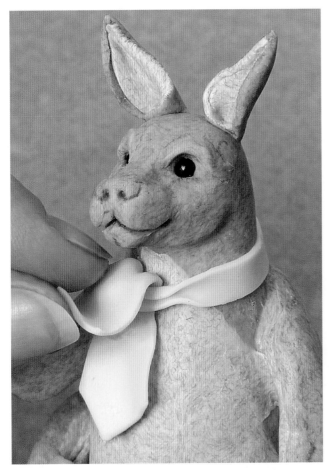

Fold the top half of the scarf down over the joint in the neckband.

Beret. The beret (artist hat) is made of three colors. The hatband is a flat yellow strip ¼" wide and 2½" long. The marbled black and purple top (shown just below the balls) is made from a ⅜" ball of purple and a ⅜" ball of black. Roll the two balls into ropes that are the same length. Twist the ropes together then form them back into a ball.

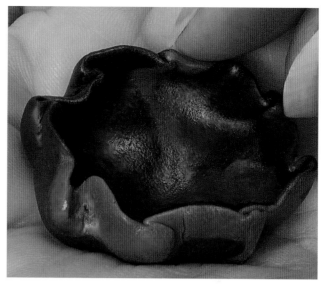

Flatten the marbled ball into a 1¾" circle by alternately pinching and rotating the clay. Work from the center out and slightly overlap the pinched areas. Work several times around the circle to achieve the size you'll need. There will be a different color pattern on each side.

Place the flattened, marbled circle in the palm of your hand then curl and crimp the edges to create a bowl shape.

Join the ends of the hatband and attach the edges of the top of the hat to one edge of the band. Curl and bend the top of the hat until you can make them fit.

Use a knife to cut a slit for the ear to go through. Roll the edges open with a pointed dowel or knitting needle and slide it over the ear.

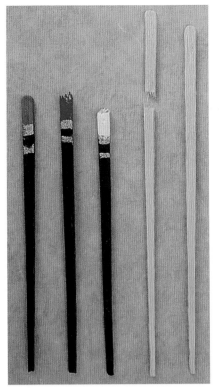

Trim the brush handles to the desired length and place in pouch. Push them into the unbaked clay of the pouch to hold them in place, but be careful not to poke through.

Paintbrushes. The paintbrushes are not made of clay. They are flat toothpicks broken to the desired lengths and painted with acrylic paint; the longest one is 2¾". You will need four brushes: three for the pouch and one for the hand.

STEP 12 FINAL BAKE

Make a final check of accessories and positioning. If a tiny spot of super glue will help secure something, use it. Be sure the hat is down on the head, the paintbrushes are in the hand and pouch, and the paint palette is in the other hand with one finger through the hole and one edge braced on the pouch. (The palette may need a prop like the one used for Mama Bear's pie so it won't droop.) Now brace Kerri carefully on all sides so things cannot shift and bake at 250° F for 30 minutes. Cool in the oven.

Dexter Dalmatian, Firedog

Every firehouse needs a mascot, and Dexter Dalmatian is right there to guard his position. He has a big job and a big name to match it. His coat is open and his boots are rolled down, but he is always ready to go when the fire alarm sounds.

Dexter uses many of the same techniques as Kerri Kangaroo. His armature is a bit smaller and slightly flattened on the sides. Dexter's nose is longer and more slender and will not require the extra clay on his muzzle. You will have two new fun items added to this project: glow-in-the dark clay for the reflective bands on the coat and hat, and spots made with waterbased acrylic paint.

Since there are so many pieces required for this project, they will be shown and described as they are needed rather than at the beginning.

You will also need a no. 3 round paintbrush and either black or dark gray acrylic paint.

USING WHITE CLAY

White can be difficult to work with because it gets dirty easily and picks up traces of other clays left on your tools, work surface and hands. After using dark colors, wash your hands with soap and wipe the work area with a clean paper towel. If you use a pasta machine, clean the bottom of the rollers and separator blades with a paper towel. Do not use water; it isn't necessary and will rust your pasta machine.

I USED THESE COLORS

FIMO Soft: Black, White, Lemon, Indian Red, Metallic Gold, Metallic Silver and a 50/50 mix of Caramel and Sahara

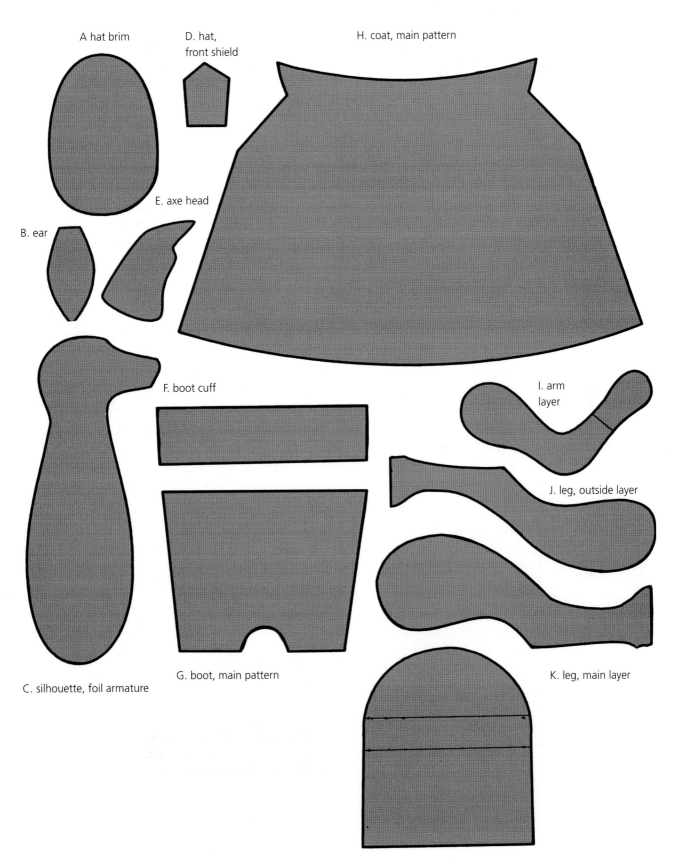

A hat brim

D. hat,
front shield

H. coat, main pattern

E. axe head

B. ear

F. boot cuff

I. arm
layer

J. leg, outside layer

C. silhouette, foil armature

G. boot, main pattern

K. leg, main layer

L. coat sleeve

STEP 1   MAKE PARTS TO START DEXTER'S BODY

- foil armature – 12" x 16" piece of foil crushed to fit silhouette pattern C; flatten sides so the body is ¾" wide
- white body shell – 3½" square, ⅛" thick
- eyelid – white crescents slightly more than ⅟₁₆" thick, cut with ³⁄₁₆" circle cutter
- ears – pattern B in white clay, ⅟₁₆" thick
- tail – tapered white rope 1½" long, ¼" thick at wide end and ⅛" thick at tip

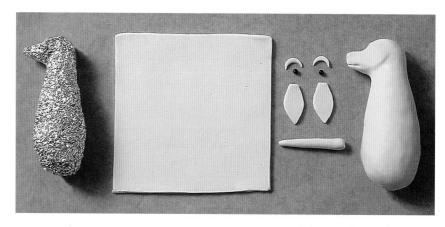

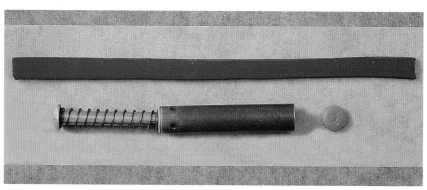

The collar is ⅛" wide, 3" long and just over ⅟₁₆" thick. The circle is the same thickness cut with the ³⁄₁₆" cutter. I used FIMO Soft Metallic Gold for the medallion.

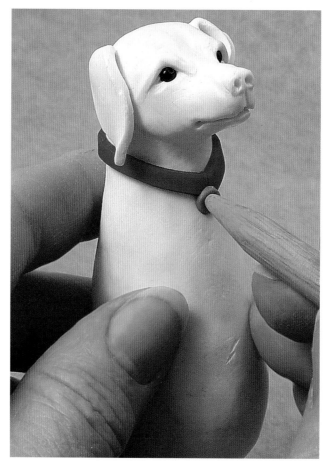

Wrap the collar so it is higher in the back, and trim the ends to match in the front. Attach the round medallion.

Following the same procedures used for Kerri Kangaroo, cover the armature and roll it smooth. Set and blend the eyes and eyelids. Shape the nose, cut the mouth and round its corners. To add the ears, s nd the ear up and slant it slightly to the back. Use the rounded end of your dowel to gently cup the base of the ear into the head, joining the two. Then fold the ear down and a little forward.

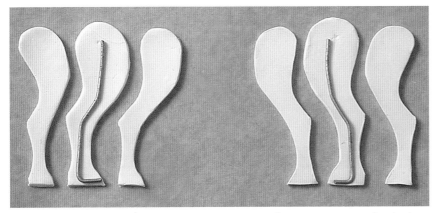

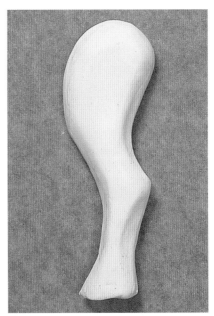

The legs are three ⅛" layers of white with a 2½" piece of 14-gauge wire sandwiched between the two inside layers. Place the ¼" foot bend at the end of the wire at the bottom of the clay to keep Dexter from leaning forward. Use patterns K and J for the leg pieces.

STEP 2 MAKE THE BOOTS

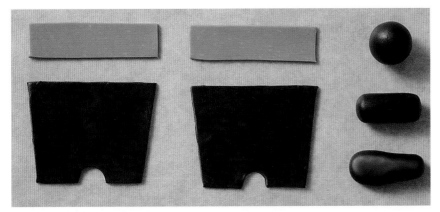

Each boot is made in three parts. Start with a ⅜" ball of black, and roll it into a 1" long rope. Flatten one end into a wedge shape like the toe of a shoe. Pinch the other end to narrow the heel. It may help to look at your own shoe or boot. Use patterns F (Sahara plus Caramel) and G (Black) with ¹⁄₁₆" thick clay to make the upper boot.

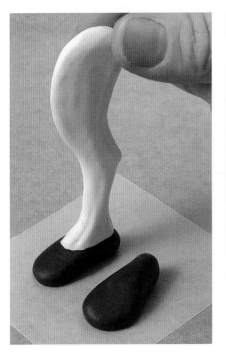

Attach the paw to the boot shoe, and wrap it with the upper boot. The cuff should be attached before it is placed on the leg. Take care to keep the lower cuff from sticking to the boot.

The boot ends should butt, not overlap. The cuff remains open, so do not join the ends. Smooth and reshape the heel. Attach the legs to the body. You may want a joint wrap to fill the deepest part of the crease between the leg and the body. This will help stabilize the legs. (You used joint wraps to fill the deep grooves between Papa Bear's legs and body.) Attach the tail at both ends. Attaching it to the boot will reduce its risk of getting broken. Place Dexter on your baking surface, and balance him so he stands alone. Brace him so he can't shift or fall during baking.

STEP 3   MAKE THE AXE AND HAT

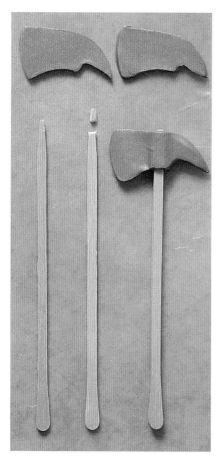

The handle of the axe is two sandwich picks (much larger than flat toothpicks) glued together and shortened to 3¼". Shorten from the narrow end. The handle is layered between two clay axe heads and baked for 20 minutes. Use pattern E and ¹⁄₁₆" thick FIMO Soft Metallic Silver clay to make the axe head.

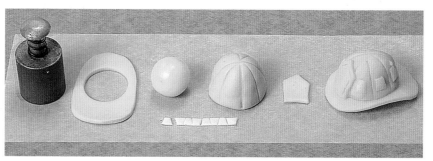

For the hat you need: ¾" circle cutter, patterns A and D for hat brim and shield, FIMO Soft Lemon Yellow clay slightly thicker than ¹⁄₁₆" and a ⅝" Lemon Yellow ball of clay. The safety reflectors are FIMO Soft Nightglow, cut from a band ¹⁄₁₆" thick and ¼" wide. The base of each reflector is ³⁄₁₆" wide.

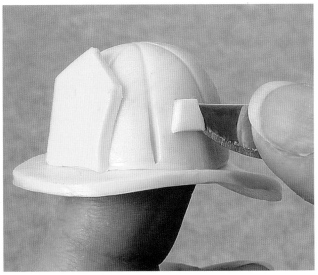

Hollow the top of the hat with a rounded dowel, and mark lines with the back of your knife blade. Fit the top of the hat onto the brim and press gently. Turn it over and roll the brim/top seam with your dowel to bond. Support the outside with your finger. Attach the shield to the center front, and circle the hat top with reflectors. The reflectors glow in the dark, but do not reflect light.

Shape the brim and place the finished hat on your large circle cutter until it is needed. The hat can be cured in the first bake for easier handling and glued in place later. Or, you can wait until after Dexter's coat is fitted to adjust the hat to his head.

STEP 4   FIRST BAKE

Bake at 250° F for 30 minutes. Bake the axe, too, for easier handling later. If the hat is to be included, do not bake it on his head. It will stick and cause problems fitting the coat. Bake it on the large circle cutter.

STEP 5   MAKE THE SPOTS

Dexter's nose and spots are painted with a dark gray acrylic paint and a no. 3 round brush. If you mess up a spot, you can wipe or wash it off with a cotton swab before it dries. The color shown is Plaid's Folk Art Wrought Iron.

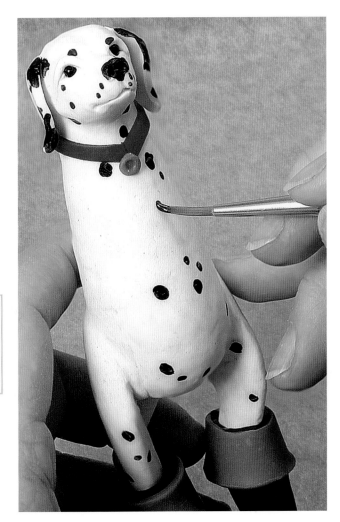

PAINTING CLAY

If you add paint to baked clay and don't like it, just wash or wipe it off before it dries. Dry the clay and try again. Polymer clay is waterproof.

STEP 6   MAKE THE ARMS

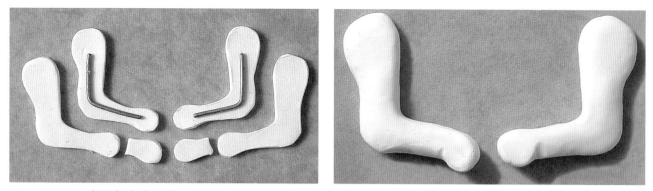

Use pattern I and ⅛" thick clay. The arms are two layers of clay with a bent 14-gauge wire (1" long) centered between them. The paws are three layers from the wrist down. Mark toes by rolling a tool around the end of the paw.

STEP 7   MAKE THE COAT

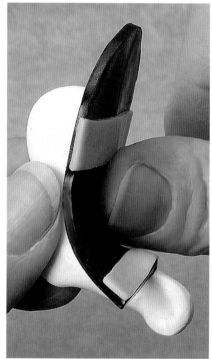

Roll a 4" x 6" sheet of Black ⅟₁₆" thick and a 2" x 6" sheet of FIMO Soft Nightglow ⅟₁₆" thick or slightly thinner (#5 on the pasta machine). Use sleeve and coat patterns H and L. The top reflector bands are ⁵⁄₁₆" wide, the bottom bands are ³⁄₁₆" wide, and the five buckles are ⅟₁₆" x ³⁄₁₆".

Center the sleeve over the front of the arm and press it back against the bend in the elbow. Wrap the sides around the arm matching the glow bands at the back.

Roll the back of your knife blade over the arm at the elbow to create wrinkles. Fold the top of the sleeve in on itself to bulk up the shoulder at the top and just above the arm.

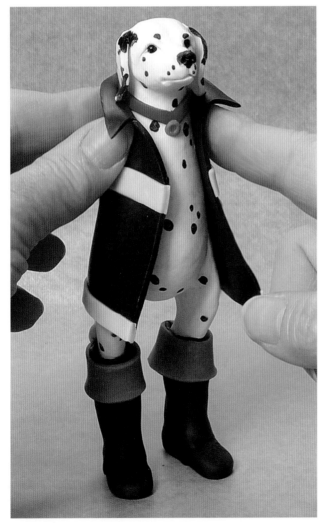

Roll the coat collar back, but not down against the coat. Center the coat on Dexter's back and press the upper back and shoulder areas hard enough to stick them to the body. Avoid the reflector band on the back so it will not be crushed or smeared. A drop of glue on his upper back and arm area will help, but is not necessary.

STEP 8   ATTACH THE ARMS, AXE AND HAT

Lift the collar slightly and press the arms onto the coat. Put them toward the back of each side. Roll the top of the shoulders to flatten them, and mend the seam between them and the body. Next, fasten the hat in place. It sits on top of his ears and coat collar and does not come down over much of his head. Put Dexter on a baking surface. Place the axe under his paw and press hard enough to hold the axe in place. Brace him on all sides and bake for 30 minutes at 250° F. Cool in the oven. To make the boots shiny, coat them with FIMO gloss varnish or Sculpey gloss glaze after cooling.

Paddy Police Dog

Paddy's life as a police dog is often very complicated. Much of his of time and energy is spent tending to tiny details. Things that look simple often require more attention than we can guess.

Paddy is the most complex project in this book. His head requires intricate modeling, and his uniform and accessories are detailed. He will be baked three times to protect your work at various stages. He will also introduce you to a new way of constructing an arm and adding delicate color effects with powdered colorants such as rouge and eyeshadow.

Pieces required for each step will be shown and described as they are needed. There are also patterns for you to trace and cut out to use as templates.

> ### I USED THESE COLORS
> FIMO Soft: Jasper, Black, Windsor Blue, White, Metallic Gold and Metallic Silver

STEP 1 MAKE THE PARTS TO START PADDY

All these pieces are a 50/50 blend of Jasper and White:

- armature – 12" x 18" piece of foil crushed to fit pattern I
- body shell – 3½" square, ⅛" thick
- ears – ⅛" thick, pattern M
- eyelid – ¹⁄₁₆" thick crescents cut with ⅜" circle cutter
- eyes – 3mm black beads
- ruff – three pieces ⅛" thick, patterns K and L

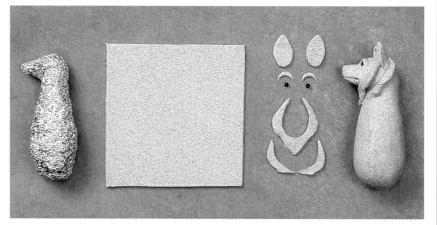

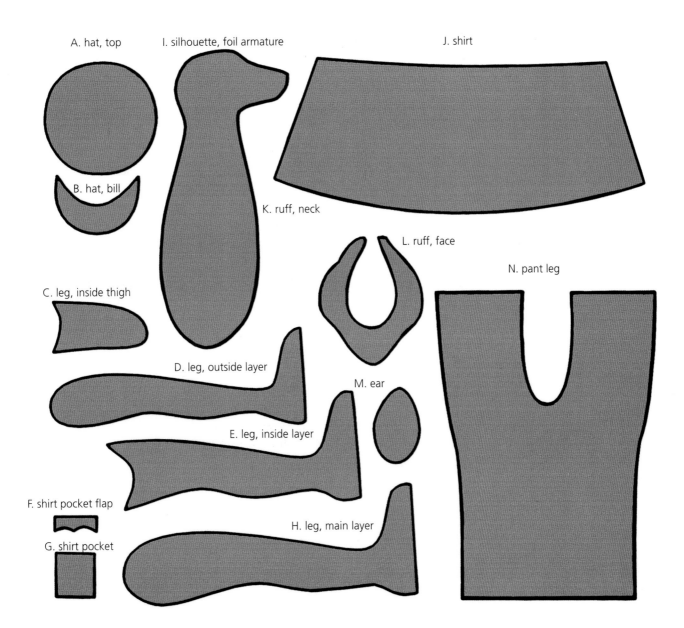

A. hat, top

I. silhouette, foil armature

J. shirt

B. hat, bill

K. ruff, neck

L. ruff, face

N. pant leg

C. leg, inside thigh

D. leg, outside layer

M. ear

E. leg, inside layer

F. shirt pocket flap

G. shirt pocket

H. leg, main layer

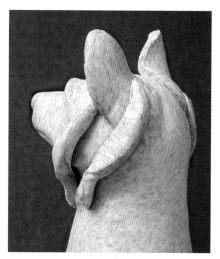

From the front, note the ear shape and angle, facial features and positioning of the large ruff piece.

The left side of the head shows the ear attachment and location of one of the smaller ruff pieces. Notice the top (narrowest end) of the ruff crosses the lower part of the ear.

You can see the top of both of the small ruff pieces.

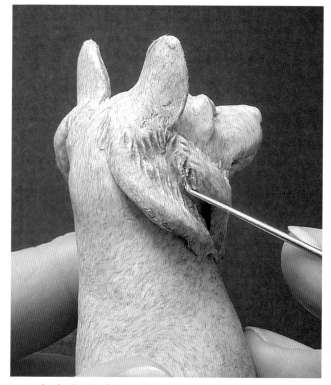

Start refining the ruff by texturing and blending the seams. Work from the ears to the bottom of the chin. Think about the shape you want the ruff to be; nudge or shift it into position as you go. Do this to all three ruff pieces. Texturing can be done by pressing with a toothpick tip, a needle tool, the back of a knife blade or a dental tool.

Now do the back of the ruff, pulling, pushing and nudging the clay to fill gaps, hide seams and create new hairy shapes.

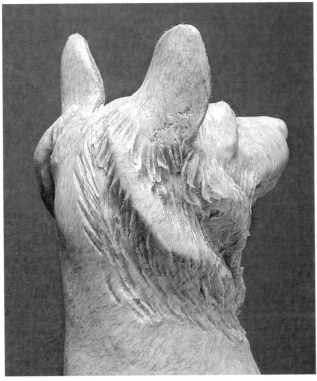

With the front and the back seams of the ruff textured, Paddy looks and feels much more like a dog. Notice the top ridge on the ruff is still smooth.

For this step, use a dental tool (some craft stores have tools like them) or a narrow wire like a paperclip or quilting pin bent at a sharp angle. Texture an irregular groove through the remaining smooth, flat surfaces on the ruffs. Remember this is hair, not rows of corn. Make some cuts deeper or wavy.

STEP 3   COLOR WITH EYESHADOW

Eyeshadow applied with a soft-bristle paintbrush is a wonderful way to add subtle color variations to your clay. Dust the muzzle, front edge and back of the ears, the back of the head and top of the ruff with dark gray eyeshadow. Build the color a little at a time. It is easy to put more on but nearly impossible to remove it. Brush the surface gently—don't pound it in and make it blotchy. Use rust, rose or a warm earthy eyeshadow inside the ears, under the eyes and along the sides of the nose. Powdered rouge will also work. Make the strongest concentration at the bottom of the ears and back of the muzzle close to the eye. Paint the nose with dark gray or black acrylic paint.

STEP 4   MAKE THE LEGS

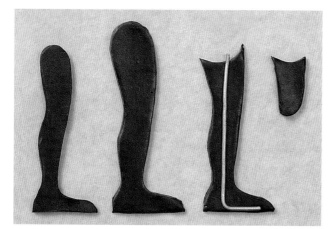 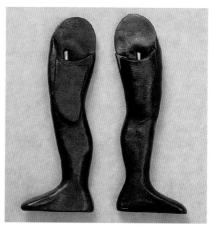

Paddy has a human-shaped leg. It is four layers of clay ⅛" thick (patterns C, D, E and H). The leg armature is made of 14-gauge wire 3" long. The foot bend is ½" long. The wire is sandwiched between layers E and H. Layers E and C are the inside of the leg.

There are no muscle grooves. The finished leg is smooth and the edges rounded. If the foot looks too skinny, add another thickness of clay to the inside front third of it.

STEP 5   FIRST BAKE

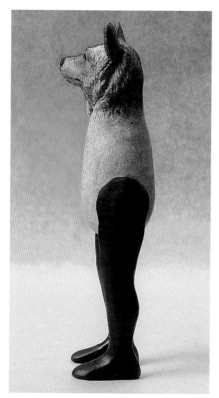

Center the legs on the body, and smooth the joint ridges around the leg. Place Paddy on your baking surface and balance him to stand. Brace him from all sides. Bake for 40 minutes in preheated 265° F oven.

STEP 6   MAKE THE PANTS

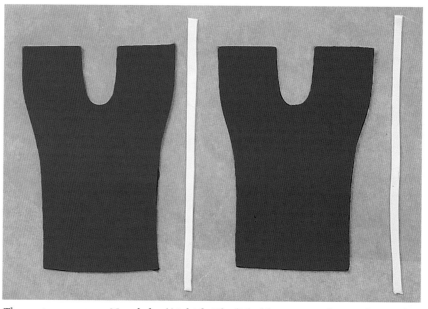

The pants use pattern N and clay 1/16" thick. The light blue stripe is thinner (#5 on the pasta machine) and ⅛" wide. The stripe and the shirt are the same color: eight parts White with one part Windsor Blue (pants color). Roll and knead until you have a uniform blend with no streaks. To make it simple, use one-half of a new block of white and a ⅜" ball of blue.

 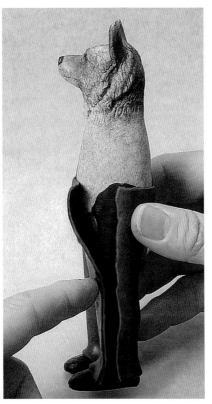 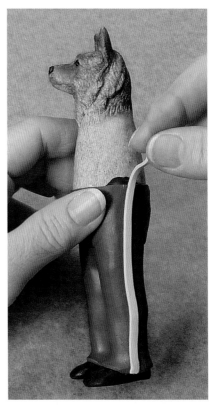

Make two body wraps with the pants color and fill the groove around the inside of the thighs. Roll the wraps with a dowel to make an arch from the thigh to the center of the crotch. Put the U at the top of the pants between the legs and attach at the center of the front and back.

Wrap the sides around the leg and butt the edges on the outside of the leg. Don't worry if it doesn't fit tightly. Wrinkles are OK too, pants do wrinkle. If the pants are too small, gently stretch the clay. Match the lower edges of the pant leg.

Cover the outside seam with the light blue stripe. Trim the bottom to match the hem. Trim the top of the pants to make a smooth, blunt line around the body. Leave a blunt cut.

To protect your work brace and bake for 10 minutes at 265° F.

STEP 8   MAKE THE SHIRT

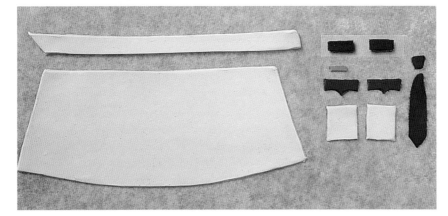

Use patterns J, F and G for the shirt and pockets. The shirt, collar and cuffs are ⅟₁₆" thick; all other pieces are slightly thinner (#5 on the pasta machine). The shoulder tabs are ⅛" x ¼", and the tiny metallic gold is a name bar ⅟₁₆" x ¼". The tie is ¼" x 1" and the knot is a ³⁄₁₆" square. The bottom of the knot-square will be rolled around the edges of the tie.

 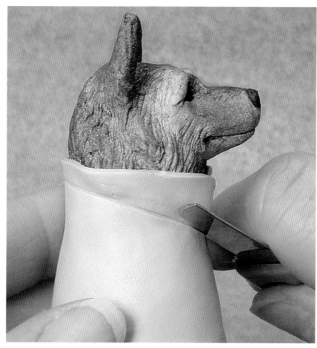

Butt the shirt against the top of the pants. Attach the shirt at the center of the front, wrap the body, and butt the edges together. Trim or stretch the clay to fit.

Press the shirt smoothly against the body to remove air pockets. Trim the neck. The rest of the shirt will be detailed after the arms are attached.

STEP 9   MAKE THE POLICE UNIFORM ACCESSORIES

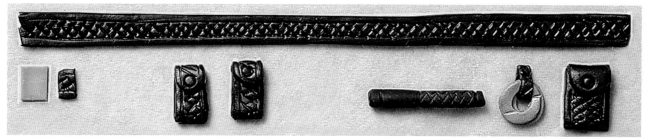

The belt and two smallest pouches can be made from the same black band of clay ¼" x 6". Surface details are made with the back of a knife blade. The small pouch requires 1" of clay. The large pouch requires a piece ½" x 1¼". The metallic gold clay buckle is ³⁄₁₆" x ¼", with the black overlay slightly smaller. You will make the nightstick and handcuffs later. Make the belt. Attach it at the front, centering it over the seam between the pants and shirt. Wrap it around the body, gently pressing it onto the unbaked shirt clay. Trim and cover the cut with the buckle.

The pouches (and belt) have cross-hatch detailing. Cut one end of the band flat and the other rounded. Fold the flat end up, keeping enough of the round end exposed to fold down for the top flap. Imprint a circle for the snap fastener with the end of a retractable ballpoint pen case.

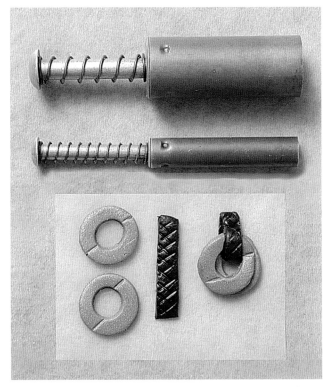

The handcuffs are metallic silver circles cut with the ⅜" and ³⁄₁₆" circle cutters. The strap that attaches them to the belt is ⅛" x ½".

The nightstick is a ⅛" x 1" rope with cross hatching on lower half and three grooves rolled with the back of your knife.

You will need two badges, one for the hat and one for the shirt. They require three silver circles cut with the ³⁄₁₆" circle cutter, one and one-half circles and a tiny strip or rope for each badge. Make the depression in the circle with a small brush handle.

The hat may take some practice. The hat and trim are ¹⁄₁₆" thick. Use patterns A and B for the circles and bill. The hole in the bottom circle is cut with the ¾" circle cutter. The hatband is ¼" x 2¾". The gold metallic band is ¹⁄₁₆" x ¾". The tiny pieces at the ends of the gold band are cut from scrap and will be rolled into balls to cover and decorate the ends once the band is attached to the hat.

Join the hatband and attach it to the top of the bill. Offset the bottom circle so it is on top of the hatband in the front. At the back, attach it to the vertical outside edge. Attach the top circle along the front first and stretch to fit. Now add the gold trim and the badge.

STEP 10 MAKE THE ARMS AND FINISH THE SHIRT

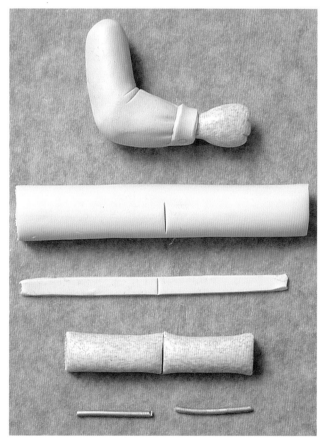

Think in pairs the way you did in the beginner projects. The sleeves are made from a rope ½" in diameter and 3" long. The cuffs are ⅛" wide, 2" long and ¹⁄₁₆" thick. The paws are made from a ⅜" x 1" rope and will have a ¾" 14-gauge wire armature.

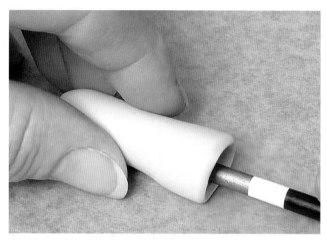

Cut the arm rope in half and round one end of each piece. Support the sides of the flat end between your thumb and forefinger, and push a brush handle straight into the end. Twist the handle as you push to drill in about half an inch. Lay the sleeve on your work surface, and use the brush as a rolling pin to open the hole enough to insert the arm. Rotate the sleeve as you roll to keep the sleeve an even thickness on all sides. Cut the paw coil in half and round on end of each piece. Place the center of the coil between your fingers and roll to make the wrist. Texture the paws. Push a fat needle into the end of the arm and deep enough to go into the paw. Remove the needle and insert the arm wire.

FINISH THE ARM AND SLEEVE
Place half of the arm into the sleeve opening and close the sleeve around it. Use the end of a toothpick to press in wrinkles. Bend the arm before wrapping the cuff around the wrist to cover the bottom of the sleeve. Trim the cuff so there is a slight overlap. Use the tip of the pen case to imprint a button.

Attach the arms at the shoulder. Let the arm that will hold the hat angle out to the side away from the body. Roll the top of the arms with a dowel to flatten the shoulders and press on the shoulder tabs. Now attach the pockets, tie, nametag and badge. The pocket pleats are pressed in with the back of your knife before the top flap is added and the buttons imprinted.

Start with the pointed end and attach the collar. Trim the other point; it needs to be nearly straight down. Do not press the bottom of the collar onto the shoulders.

STEP 11 ADD THE FINISHING DETAILS

Add the knot to the top of the tie. Place the finished hat under the arm, and press the arm down and in to hold the hat in place. Press the two small pouches onto the belt front.

Put the large pouch as close to the arm and hat as possible. Add the nightstick and handcuffs. If the nightstick is bent or wavy, straighten it. A tiny bit of instant glue can be used to stick the handcuffs to the back of the baked pants. Imprint the strap snap with a ballpoint pen case.

STEP 12 FINAL BAKE

Take a final look at Officer Paddy from each side before he is braced again for his final bake of 25 minutes at 260° F. Cool in the oven. To make the shoes shiny, paint them with FIMO gloss varnish or Sculpey gloss glaze after cooling

List of Suppliers

Manufacturers of Polymer Clay

American Art Clay Co., Inc.
4717 W. 16th Street
Indianapolis, IN 46222-2598
Telephone: (800) 374-1600
Fax: (317) 248-9300
http://www.amaco.com
Manufacturer of polymer clay, millefiori canes and push molds. Importer of FIMO and FIMO Soft. Also sells polymer clay tools, books and videos.

Eberhard Faber GmbH
P.O. Box 1220
D-92302 Neumarkt/Germany
Telephone: 09181/43 0-0
Fax: 09181/4 30-222
Manufacturer of FIMO and clay products.

Polyform Products Company
1901 Estes Avenue
Elk Grove Village, IL 60007-5415
Telephone: (847) 427-0020
Fax: (847) 427-0426
http://sculpey.unety.com
Manufacturer of Sculpey clay products and accessories.

T+F GmbH
LandsteinerstraBe 10
D-63303 Dreieich/Germany
Telephone: (0 61 03) 8 85 14
Fax: (90 61 03) 8 85 85
Manufacturer of Cernit clay products.

Wholesale/Retail Resources

Accent Import-Export, Inc.
P.O. Box 4361
Walnut Creek, CA 94596
Telephone: (510) 827-2889
Fax: (510) 827-0521
Importer of FIMO and FIMO Soft (and blending charts for mixing colors). Manufacturer of KaleidoKane Classic millifiori canes.

Kemper Tools and Doll Supplies
13595 12th Street
Chino, CA 91710
Telephone: (800) 388-5367
Fax: (909) 627-4008
Specializes in wholesale and retail tools, pattern cutters and Cernit.

Wee Folk Creations
18476 Natchez Avenue
Prior Lake, MN 55372
Telephone (612) 447-3828
Fax: (612) 447-8816
http://www.weefolk.com
Specializes in Cernit, FIMO, FIMO Soft, Sculpey, Super Sculpey, Premo! push molds, books and videos.

Index